MOOSE MEDICINE

Healing Wisdom from the Natural World

ROBYN BRIDGES

Balboa Press books may be ordered through booksellers or by contacting:

Balboa Press
A Division of Hay House
1663 Liberty Drive
Bloomington, IN 47403
www.balboapress.com
1-(877) 407-4847

Because of the dynamic nature of the Internet, any web addresses or links contained in this book may have changed since publication and may no longer be valid. The views expressed in this work are solely those of the author and do not necessarily reflect the views of the publisher, and the publisher hereby disclaims any responsibility for them.

The author of this book does not dispense medical advice or prescribe the use of any technique as a form of treatment for physical, emotional, or medical problems without the advice of a physician, either directly or indirectly. The intent of the author is only to offer information of a general nature to help you in your quest for emotional and spiritual well-being. In the event you use any of the information in this book for yourself, which is your constitutional right, the author and the publisher assume no responsibility for your actions.

Printed in the United States of America

ISBN: 978-1-4525-6984-0 (sc)
ISBN: 978-1-4525-6986-4 (hc)
ISBN: 978-1-4525-6985-7 (e)

Library of Congress Control Number: 2013904020

Balboa Press rev. date: 6/26/2013

for the wildness

❧

and the wilderness

❧

in all of us

Table of Contents

Introduction

Once again I am strolling along the river's edge in Montana's backcountry, seeking solace from life's disappointments. With any luck, soon I will happen upon a moose, seeing just the top of his long dusty-brown muzzle wrapping deftly around streamside branches as he breaks them off to chew. The damp and sheltering willows will camouflage the rest of his massive body. I know I can spot one if only by a lone willow whose top branches will wiggle with the thrill of the huge creature feeding off them. I will wiggle too, with the thrill of such danger and awkward beauty so close to my own. I am kin here to some ineffable knowing deep in my bones. Here, my sorrows quiet. Here, I belong.

Perhaps if my young adult life had not derailed so completely, I might never have discovered the restorative power of nature. I would never have hiked so far into the mountains alone and caught my breath as I rounded a bend and came face to face with a majestic moose. If I hadn't lost my family, I might never have realized that I could pour my heartache into the winding stream that sustains the life of the magnificent four-legged, awkward creatures who revived my will to live.

Years ago, as a newly married young college graduate full of faith in my future and in God, I had only one dream: to create my own happy family. Every fiber of my being knew I could raise children with positivity, not like my own mother had, not with negative words and slaps and fingernails digging into my wrists to yank me here or there. But infertility and an increasingly infertile marriage began to gnaw at my soul. I had hoped that I might poultice my discontent with the adoption of three young children. Yet a few years later, as the children's own wounds forced them from our home back into special care, I found myself divorced and entirely shunned by family, friends, and pastors. I was unemployed, faithless, and broke.

Almost instinctively, I moved toward the one constant I intuited I could trust: the safe mountains surrounding my Montana home, where possibly a new god might dwell. During those years, I lugged the disappointment withering my heart into long days of hiking and sighing. Once a former weekend backpacker, I now contented myself with day trips sandwiched between three minimum-wage jobs. My only immediate relationship was with nature itself. I began to discover a new way of belonging. I started to hear everything in the natural world speaking to me in its own language—about itself, about me, about life. I breathed deeper. And I gratefully took it all in.

The realization that moose were becoming important teachers dawned slowly. During the first summer that witnessed my loneliness, one morning I had been aimlessly winding through willowed streamside trails. Upon rounding a sharp curve, I was amazed to see a large bull moose less than twenty feet away. I froze midstride, my fear turning to admiration. Moose! I'd never been so close to one before. Having clearly heard my loud approach, the moose's large, oblong ears were keeping me in antenna range, though his body remained at an oblique angle. He glanced my way only briefly, being more interested in browsing the middle of the slow-moving stream than in attacking. Sporting huge withers and in full rack, he clacked along the underwater stones while nibbling green fronds.

Gazing into his large brown eyes, watching his curiously rounded muzzle rising out of the water and descending back in, and hearing his quiet sloshing around the willow-side waters, I was captivated. He was alone and content. I leaned up against a small tree and soon hunkered down to sit on the other side of the narrow stream. Mesmerized, I began to glean something from him about the capacity to survive, even thrive, alone. His well-being infused my body and mind until my breath seemed to be his. We stayed close like that for some time, him grazing on long, green stream fronds and me transfixed, cross-legged and still.

He eventually ambled off with only one more casual glance in my direction. I breathed in air as though I'd been without it for centuries. That he was surviving so well in such solitude profoundly impacted me that day and has since informed my own ability to survive the unplanned solitariness of my own life.

This epiphany was what Native people the world over call a type of "medicine." Many indigenous tribes (some prefer to be called "nations") believe that humans can be adopted by the collective spirit of any species of animal. For example, the Grandmother Twylah, elder of the Wolf Clan of the Seneca Nation, taught me that when a person realizes a specific animal has important lessons for him or her, that animal is considered to be that person's teaching, or medicine. Though some indigenous tribes and nations are adamant about the privacy of any traditional teachings, Grandmother Twylah had a vision of the urgency to share such wisdom with all peoples. Her encouragement helped open me to the imaginal but subjectively real world of interspecies communication. I learned to invite numinous experience through an instinctive spiritual connection, including dialogue with plants, animals, and the elements of earth, wind, water, and fire. This capacity is not limited to a certain type of person or culture. Each of us can find our own unique animal "medicine" to help heal whatever ails us.

Moose specifically taught me many necessary qualities for my own life. That moose model the ability to thrive so well alone has become my greatest inspiration. "Moose Medicine" has become my guide.

In the years after my divorce, working with a brilliant therapist helped my psyche to heal. And a growing desire to help others heal in the natural world resulted in a master's degree in counseling and participation in many psycho-spiritual conferences, eco-psychology workshops, and sacred healing methods. For the next twenty-five years, I helped others who had become lost, as I had, to find their way once again by journeying into the heart of nature. In the process, they rediscovered who they really were all along: spiritual beings having a human experience, with both animal and human allies.

Many city dwellers seldom have the chance to wander boggy streams and have the kind of wild encounters I have experienced. Yet most of us living a contemporary life style, no matter where we live on the globe, can still access a quiet park or sanctuary where the earth has been fairly undisturbed. It is here that we relearn the art of listening to sentient others all around us: earth, sky, trees, plants, and animals. This is our medicine, the spiritual antidote for what ails us. Recognizing the mysterious power of the natural world to teach, renew, and restore, we learn that whatever our life challenges, even through unimaginable sorrow, spring will surely follow winter.

The chapters that follow are mapped to assist navigation of your own life challenges as you traverse your own psychological and spiritual territory. Along the way, I hope you will discover—or rediscover—guidance, inspiration, and insight through nature that you can freely apply to your own life. Part I, "The Medicine of the Elements," strolls through encounters with moose and attendant teachings from the elements of earth, wind, water, and fire. Part II, "The Medicine of Plants, Animals, and Place," winds through paths with animal, plant, and geographic locations that prompt a variety of ecological and healing realizations. Part III, "The Medicine of Two-Leggeds," explores humans' true place in nature and seeks practical ways to live more naturally with ourselves and others based on the ways that nature organizes itself.

Through reading *Moose Medicine,* I hope you will be inspired to get up-close and personal with nature or to return to doing so if you have strayed from the practice. In the process, you may find yourself spending more contemplative time in nature, and as a result experience more of your own cadenced balance and sure steps. *Moose Medicine* seeks to wind you through the backcountry of your own consciousness, where a pristine remembrance thrives. May you track your own form of Moose Medicine well.

Part I

The Medicine of the Elements

The Universe is the Externalization of the Soul.
—Ralph Waldo Emerson

The earth, which houses my beloved moose, abounds in unabashed richness and wild diversity. From sleek rivers to timbered mountains, from echoing canyons to pounding waterfalls, through wind-swept desert and fire-swept prairie, the earth and the elements of earth, air, water, and fire offer a cornucopia for the senses and a sense of divine mystery.

The power of our life-giving elements speaks to us in contemporary culture as we negotiate political debate over air and water toxicity, or plan a vacation, or even consider what to wear to match the weather. The elements are deeply embedded in our human psyches; our ancestors had to understand and respect each one for their safety and sustenance. As a result, they developed a kind of relationship with them: rituals to assure a good harvest, oral teachings for when to plant, where animal herds move, and how to secure safe housing. They also believed they could actually hear and receive personal and community wisdom directly from the elements, teachings that would help them live both safer and more meaningful lives. Today we have lost so much of that intimate connection with the rawness of the power of these elements. Instead of being guided by oncoming winter, we see it as a bother. Instead of welcoming rain, we protect ourselves against it. A return to the insights that the elements offer helps us get back in sync with the power and essence of the natural world.

In stretching our earth-like minds to branch out into the natural world, we paradoxically grow deeper roots in our own lives. We enhance personal balance day by day through tuning into the seasonal and diurnal rhythms of the earth, listening for messages on the early morning wind, acting with the fluidity of water, and harnessing the power of fire to accomplish goals. I join with you in primal remembrance.

1

Animal Dreams

Let me notice my surroundings. Let me remember who I am.
Let me be a good animal today.
—Native teaching

As winter swirls around my safe home in the quiet mountains of southwest Montana, unplowed roads prohibit travel to my esteemed moose country. The relaxed luxury of summer tracking has become a cold reminiscence. With the onset of inclement weather and working too many hours indoors, I have once again fallen out of balance. The wild animals in my mind then go into hiding, it seems, and down forgotten canyons to wait for me to wake up and remember them. Can I call upon the memory of inspiration and sustenance I received from them in past encounters?

I let myself recall all I've felt, heard, seen, touched, and tasted in nature to bring past memory into present reality. I remember the long days of excitement and adventure I've known tramping around the mountains in my treasured state. An odd irony is that Montana is nicknamed "the treasure state," which refers to mining. I refer to the treasure of our vast, still-protected wilds.

My most recent sighting of moose happened earlier this winter, before seasonal road closures. I'd arrived at midday to my favorite cozy cabin up the west fork of the Bitterroot River in southwest Montana. Having spent the afternoon inside curled up by a wood fire in my nightgown, I was dreamily watching wisps of snow skitter along the road. In spite of the idyllic ambiance, the setting sun was heralding a sense of approaching adventure, the kind where you know that even though the light is fading, an uncertain but appealing event is about to unfold.

As oncoming night swallowed the day, something called to me. My body, not my mind, shook me from the seductive warmth of the couch and beckoned me out the door and up the road, away from my winter cabin. Already in an altered state, I pulled on a jacket over my nightgown, slipped on my winter shoes, and without gloves or hat shivered toward the north stream in the setting sun. I was alone, half-afraid, and thrilled to be moving deep into the waiting silence. Soon I was approaching a nearby group of willows close to the now deserted road, crunching snow under my unlaced boots.

Massive pine and fir trees stood all around, bravely anchoring the quiet. Now I knew what, or who, had called me. I could *feel* the presence of moose—at least one, and maybe more. I stopped and stared for many minutes into the sheltering willows, listening so hard I started to hear my own heartbeat, staring so intently that the branches began to blur.

And then, only a stone's throw across the stream from me and near an old county road, I saw him: the most perfect, healthy, robust brown three-year-old boy moose I'd ever seen, sporting his first small apologies for a rack (moose aficionados know to call these antlers *racks*). His dark auburn-brown coat sparkled brighter than the snow, and his eyes had none of the older bull moose's "God, you're annoying me" look, but held a new, curious interest. I smiled and sighed at him several times, the way you would to a new lover.

I begged whatever god might care that the upcoming late-winter hunting permits would not affect him. He would be such an easy shot, there by the road and so trusting. I almost wanted to scare him away so he would flee from the next human he saw. But I couldn't. Selfishly, I had to allow him to become comfortable with me, to take him in at such close quarters: his pungent smell, the shine in his unusually large eyes, his beautifully rounded muzzle. Then I saw *her*, and laughed aloud.

She'd been standing even closer to me than he was in the willows the whole time, her lighter-brown round body holding perfect stillness as camouflage. This must be his mother. She was healthy and large, though her coat was rougher, and her belly showed what must be the eighth or ninth baby coming soon in her clearly long career. Before I could even adjust to this treat, I heard her grunt-woof and saw her ears swivel slightly toward the direction of a slight depression in the willows only a few yards away from her. There came junior, a first-year baby, toddling toward her as if just up from a late afternoon nap. She began nudging him away from the three-year-old with her long, rounded muzzle, as if not wanting these probable siblings to interact with each other. Protective as always, she kept one eye on the young bull and one on me. Soon satisfied that neither of us was going to be a problem, she began to graze, reaching the tops of the highest willows. Her baby tottered patiently beside her.

Though it is somewhat rare to find an entire family wintering together, and particularly rare for a mother cow to allow a young bull to stay on, there it was. They were with each other as old familiars, with the kind of comfortable and irritated interaction any family knows. And I was being accepted as a part of their end-of-day foraging. In that moment, I keenly felt my own lack of regular connection with family, and I was aware of the physical and emotional miles that lay between us. Yet here, even as an outsider, somehow I fully belonged, even if just for the moment. I felt myself caught between heaven and earth, immersed in the deep miracle of wildlife all around. Time stopped and expanded all at once. I was swept into an eternal flow of understanding and relatedness. Home could be found everywhere, but nowhere more than here.

Minutes later, it was with palpable regret that I decided I'd intruded on the family of moose long enough and backed away slowly, only then aware of my numbed feet and hands. As the last fingers of light slid away from the mountain peaks, I slowly retreated back to my warm cabin. I'd had my fix, that urge to know I could be accepted as a part of the natural wild. I was imbibing the spirit of place and moose, drinking it in to slake my incessant thirst, to reassure my loneliness that it could be in the company of a moose who, while alone, was surely not lonely. I had been seen and allowed to stay in the presence of the animals I was growing to love, oddly safe in the certainty that I could also be killed by them. Perhaps they perceived that I wished them no harm. Or perhaps the hand of the divine was opening to allow me to find my safety in belonging to the wild.

That night, as darkness wrapped itself around the valley and covered my cabin like a sheltering hand, I snuggled in to sleep, my hooves securely tucked under me, dreaming good dreams my human self can't seem to recall, but my animal self surely does.

2

Sound Bites

The only real meaning in life is the experience of it.
—Mark Salzman

Autumn morning breezes nudge me toward the deep woods on the slopes of the Bangtail Mountains near Bozeman, Montana. They are a lovely and rather shy range, engulfed by their more dramatic cousins to the west, the Bridger Mountains. Yet this very understated beauty is what draws me to them. I relish crunching alone through fallen and silent lodgepole pines. Wild lupine and Indian paintbrush and little white carpet flowers are seasonally fading in number but not in audacity. My feet follow their own whims, dodging downed timber and climbing angled logs off-trail while I peer off in the distance through the high clouds like a hawk searching for food. However, most of what I view is only more patches of forest crested with shaded outlines of undulating mountains. The standing trees close to me catch my attention, and I think I feel them pulsing with their own wonder. I greet them one by one, bowing to some, wrapping my arms around others. My heart beats slower, matching the trees' ancient rhythm. "Hello, my brothers! I am here!" I grin a bit self-consciously, even though I'm the only human around, probably for miles. They simply nod and sigh in hushed acquiescence.

The trail I've been obliquely following abruptly ends, but I am unready to go back. I proceed toward the uncharted, narrow deer trails in the woods, picking my way gradually uphill. I take careful and measured steps. A doe and her yearling startle me by moving into view and disappearing over the ridge ahead of me, departing with an echoing crunch of leaves. I stand watching them long after they are gone, their images still floating in the vacant place where they passed. The sun, in full glory, moves directly overhead. My pace increases almost beyond my will and my breath quickens as I seem to be intent on getting somewhere, nowhere, uphill, downhill, farther into the welcoming arms of these mountains and pines.

As I drop down into a deep river canyon, the river sounds increase with every step. I round a corner, and the breath catches in my throat. A dark-brown bull moose only ten yards ahead is slowly disappearing around a bend in a widening section of stream. I utter a low "aaah" of delight. He is wet and playfully shakes the fronds of riverweeds dripping from his mouth. They sway to the rhythm of his gait. He is purposefully moving upstream, where there is an even larger pond of greens. He sloshes comfortably through the murky river bottom, scratching his full paddles against branches that overhang the river. They make a scritching, hollow noise, one I intend to remember for future tracking. He does not seem to mind my presence; I think he has heard and seen me coming for quite some time. He snurfles a bit through his wide nostrils, seemingly more to clear them than to scold me. I am thrilled to be in his book of memory. As he disappears around the streambed, I decide not to pursue him. Today I just take everything as it comes.

I wave goodbye to him, fingers extended toward the heavens. I lilt on through a grassy meadow and then into the woods of downed timber. I cover another three or four miles on this carefree day, thinking of nothing and looking at everything: the small patch of blue-berried juniper, the decaying stump, the late-season Indian paintbrush fading fast. Around a steep corner, I find a small patch of open ground with sunlight streaming into it. Here my body begins to seize its own life once again, this time turning me in dizzying circles while my arms stretch wide. The noonday sun and crisp, blue air dance my feet upon patches of grass and dusty ground. A sudden self-consciousness causes me to open my eyes and check the landscape for intruders, but I only spy a nuthatch viewing my reverie, and he is busy dancing himself. After some time, my turning slows. I spy a tall, craggy stump full of moss and decaying wood; it beckons me, and I crawl into its softened arms. For a while I look upward, gazing at the white puffy clouds drifting over the blue canvas sky. Soon my eyes drift shut, and I am breathing the slumber of the forest.

Crack! I bolt upright, shivering. Adrenaline flashes through my face and feet. White peals of thunder reverberate through the now-darkened woods. The blackened skies release rain in driving pellets. The bull moose I saw earlier has returned, but upon seeing my sudden movement, he glides quickly back through the meadow. His nostrils enlarged, he flaps his ears noisily before he disappears between the armies of firs and pines.

More thunder strikes in harsh tones nearby. Ten seconds of downpour and I am already soaked. While clambering to my feet, I am momentarily struck with indecision, fretting over which route will get me away the fastest from the unwelcome lightning. Uphill into the woods could provide shelter, but it is too rigorous to climb and will take me further away from where I parked. Downhill is the only way to get back to my car. The downhill slide wins. Mile after mile, cold, drenching rain claims the heat from my body. The wet and muddy forest floor slows my running steps, inviting me to stop, curl up in some tree again, and still the growing numbness in my limbs for a while, just a while ... It would be so easy.

I catch my faulty thoughts and hurry on, leaving death and hypothermia behind. Isn't this just like me, falling headlong into some pleasure I can't resist, ignoring possible danger (like hiking alone without bad weather gear), and then being surprised by the consequences. Pleasure intoxicates me—its intimate sounds, the "ohh" of a touch, a look, a longing to hear from the forest that I am really all right, that I am connected, that I am alive. Desire has once again eclipsed common sense and I remember my willful ignorance of the smell of coming rain earlier in the day. I am fortunate when the risks I take do not outweigh the gain.

Too many fallen trees bar a quick escape. I catch my dragging shoelace on a snag and stumble, wrenching my ankle. *Oh shit, oh damn.* Hard breath echoes in my ears and sweat runs down my tensing muscles. I hear a loud thubbing noise and am sure I am being pursued by a moose, or a mountain lion. Anything could happen when my mind regresses to my fearful child self. With chagrin and an ill-afforded laugh, I realize it is only my heart beating in my ears.

Every step counts. The trail leads me back into the now-soggy open meadow with no shelter. My body is the only attractor for those white-hot strikes. The lightning will make no effort to avoid me. Gasping and gulping air, I make it to the far end of the meadow. A fast downhill scramble carries me into more trees and farther from the crashing electricity. Now I have the luxury of slowing a bit, and so does my breath. I begin to castigate myself for hiking so far in alone. My drenched boots squish mud with every step I take. Picking my way to the edge of the woods, I gratefully spy the trail and then trudge the remaining miles through the rain back to my waiting vehicle.

My Jeep looks ridiculously clean compared to my mud-speckled body and caked hiking boots. I peel off all the clothes I can, pulling on the dry T-shirt and jeans I keep in my vehicle just in case. As I slip the key into the ignition, the radio blares a country western song about how "you should have known better," and I wince. A local news bulletin breaks in and reports a rescue team searching for a lone hiker last seen before the storm only one ridge over from where I just escaped.

Nevertheless, I am a slow learner. I am already planning my next day off and where I will explore. Pulling out of the parking area and heading for home, I am still flooded with memories of the day's intoxicating early welcome as I first approached the pungent, whispering edge of the waiting woods; in particular, the lightning that spared me and the bull moose in whose life I am now recorded through the rivers of gifted memory.

3

Buffalo Ribs

I had an experience I can't prove. But everything I know ... tells me it was real. I was part of something wonderful, something that changed me forever; a vision of the Universe that tells us how tiny, and insignificant, and rare, and precious we all are. A vision that tells us we belong to something greater than ourselves. That we are not, that not one of us is, alone.

—Carl Sagan

Through the dense fog, I was looking for moose, live moose. I longed for the precious medicine of knowledge and release they had so freely proffered when I was fresh from my divorce. Three years later I was still trolling for moose to either solve my loneliness or at least to offer the comfort of their presence while I worked through guilt and sorrow. I was feeling lost and alone, stuck in grief over the biological children I never had and the adopted children who were not bonding. But you never know what you'll find when you're seeking. That overcast day in early autumn, I was to realize the truth in John Lennon's statement, "Life is what happens to you while you're busy making other plans."

For several hours I sloshed through the river bottoms just outside the north boundaries of Yellowstone Park, hoping to hear the splash or tread of a moose's wide hooves, the "woof" of a protective mother, the scraping of a bull's antler paddles against a sturdy tree. Hours passed with no luck. Discouraged, I decided to let my shoes dry a bit by hiking up to a sunnier plateau above the willow bottoms I'd been combing.

Climbing slowly through the dissipating fog, I began to truly relax my expectation of having a moose encounter. As I did, I came upon a trail with a panoramic view of the curling river and shallow ponds below. I realized the only way to enjoy my time was to give in to the day as it unfolded. I accepted that my medicine that morning was to not find moose. Perhaps instead I could let nature just show me whatever it had to offer, even if by only spending a few pleasant hours viewing the quiet openness around me. As I strolled along toward the edge of a meadow leading to the vast expanse of paper-blue sky and sage-strewn valley, I remembered the importance of giving appreciation and not always expecting to receive. With that, I let out a long sigh and gazed down at the earth to thank it for its blessings. And there, right before me, down a steep slope, lay a series of old, whitened bones. They looked like long, narrow rib shafts, a triangle-shaped shoulder bone, and bits of long, dark, curled hair from the remains of a hide. What animal might have met its end struggling up this trying hill?

In my mind's eye, as in a kind of vision, I saw a single bison. Separated from the herd, the terrified buffalo was being chased up the hill by a persistent pack of wolves. Though old, he was heavy, getting tired, and becoming exhausted beyond survival. I saw his fall, his groans, and his heartwrenching demise as the pack of wolves ate him alive. I pondered the life of this creature that, more than any other, for centuries had given its life for the nurturance of human predators, even the gratefulness of The People, the natives here in America before the white man slaughtered both The People and their Buffalo. I saw Buffalo's wildness and imagined his own keen sense of belonging with his relations; I pictured his sure and deep imprints still recorded at the rivers' edges and in the mud bogs and hot springs dotting southwest Montana.

I stooped to pick up one of the whitened rib bones at my feet. I could almost hear it saying, "Do you recall, do you see, how we still give to you even long past our death, even past the old ways of sustenance? Remember." I breathed deeply, as though the large rib was enlarging my lungs. I held it for a long time, turning it over in my hands to absorb the medicine in it, and then returned it to its resting place. The rib reminded me to give thanks for all living things that support us and the earth's interdependent networks. I felt the essence of the original Adam—as in "bone of my bone and flesh of my flesh"—and in the moment better understood the nonreligious intent behind the story of Adam and Eve and God and even the serpent, all winding their own ways through our lives. That day, Adam was my masculine "doing," deciding to hike into nature. Eve was my intuitive self who knew that to let go was sacred. The serpent of separation tempted us to forget our belonging. But now I was remembering. And then the serpent transformed into a great connector, the uroboros, eating its own tail in the eternal cycle of life and death. My breath deepened again.

The fog, like my problems, was lifting. I grew pleasantly tired. There were no problems, not now. Just being. Choosing another way to return to my vehicle, I slid kid-style down the ridge. Tiny wildflowers under my feet dotted each moss-covered rock. In the distance, I saw a herd of bison leisurely making its way across the valley. The animals related effortlessly to one another, touching noses and shaking their massive heads. Seeing their lives lumbering along, though my own dreams of having family and children had lost the meat off their bones, I couldn't help but see how everything around me was still pulsing. Death was offering its decay to create fertile soul in my life.

I knew what had died in me, and the remembrances included love and hope. Years earlier, when my dreams and I were still young and had not yet been bleached by the relentless hardship of passing seasons, my new husband and I were ensconced in college near the eastern slopes of Rocky Mountain National Park. One afternoon, between his books and the glare of his study lamp, my husband looked over at me and asked, "Why don't we take a drive up into the park?" With a quick nod from me, soon the ice of early spring was tugging at our economy-line tires as we wound up the roads that were still empty before the tourist season.

"Are the herds down this far yet?" I asked the ranger at the park entrance, hoping that melting snows would allow us a glimpse of elk.

"Oh, no," he laughed, his lips showing a slight curl of disdain. "It's far too early. We've had no sightings."

The sun was strong and our cares light, so I was content to enjoy the scenic beauty of fir-lined slopes and crystalline snow. As we rounded a corner, though, a certain knowing suddenly seized me. "Stop!" I told my husband.

"Why?" he asked incredulously. "There's nothing special here."

"Yes there is! Right there, over the second ridge. I think there's a whole herd of elk behind it."

We couldn't even see over that second ridge, let alone the first, but he obligingly pulled off the road anyway. We strained to see or smell some sign of the dusty brown four-leggeds. "Nothing," he reiterated.

"Yes, there is," I said. "Come with me quickly. Quiet!" I was soon tramping ahead of him into the hushed woods. A mile later, when we dropped over the second ridge, we saw them: at least two hundred elk clumped in large, circular groupings, moving closer up the slope toward us. He told me he would sprint downwind and come up from the back of the herd, gently driving them toward me. Though I wanted to say no, just let them be, he lit out before I had a chance. As I waited in a grove of trees, the herd came trotting up at a strong pace, the ground shaking from their hooves. Their urine-soaked musk offended my nostrils, and at the same time I keenly felt in my body their sense of family and kinship, complete with grandparents and children and community. How I longed to run with them!

I almost got my chance. The herd veered and was upon me before they or I realized it. Then I saw it—not three feet in front of me ran a faint dusty trail from left to right, apparently one of their known paths. I had chosen to hide right beside it. As they thundered past, all I could do was lean in amazement against a small tree I hoped might protect me. Several of the elk didn't even seem to see me; others didn't notice until they were almost past. One calf startled and slowed down when he saw me, his eyes round and ears intent. The force of the herd bumped him off the path toward me within touching distance, though my hands stayed at my sides. His mother veered toward me too, nickering a rebuke to her innocent one. The baby reluctantly trotted back into the motion of the herd and rejoined the communal passing.

Long after the last straggler passed by, I remained where I was, wordless and breathless, still leaning against the tree, whose slow pulse helped mine to slow too. My mouth remained open a long time.

I didn't know then how my own longing for family would never be quite fulfilled or how short the time would be for running with my own herd. I also didn't know how much that one moment of belonging would shelter me in the days to come, feeding my spirit and seeing me through child loss. It would also have to see me through divorce, poverty, and despair. Finding the herd was an event that lodged so deep in my soul that it continues to nurture me to this day. How I knew that a herd was just over the ridge is still a mystery. When the earth takes you in, somehow you know that no matter how your life turns out, you're going to be all right.

A felt sense of a confident connection pervaded me, both that day early in my marriage and later as a single woman when I found the buffalo bones. The elk encounter introduced me to nature as a source of natural belonging; the buffalo confirmed it. With precognition about the elk, I was drawing close to the heartbeat of the wilds. With the memory of the buffalo's life and last moments, I was bringing forth a wild knowledge born long ago and running it into a thankfulness for the present stream of days. It is always a privilege to be connected with something larger than my small, self-contained life. It is always good when the world teaches and inspires you by its ineffable knowing.

4

Mountain Magic

Here nature knows us. The Earth knows us. We make our offerings … on top of hills … Our history cannot be told without naming the cliffs and mountains that have witnessed our people.

—Ruth Yinshye, Navajo

We love to name things. Naming implies a familiar, even familial relationship. "Look, over there," many Montanans will proudly point. "Those are the Tobacco Root Mountains." With that naming comes a whole host of stories and memories and relationships forged within themselves and sometimes with others. We name our mountains to bridge a gap between the unfamiliar and the familiar, between the vast and powerful unknown and that which we desire to know and claim kinship.

To name a mountain range carries a type of familial acknowledgement; When we name anything, we come into a relationship with it. It becomes, as author Alice Walker called it, a "familiar." Naming a mountain range does not mean that we know it completely. Mountains maintain a hold on mystery, and this mystery may be part of the very draw we feel, the grandeur of naming the un-nameable, as if we can lean into such greatness by association. "Yes, I've hiked the Bridgers," local Gallatin Valley residents may boast, and others who live here nod in understanding and respect, knowing at least something of what that particular range means and what it stands for, as well as the power and mystery its contours carry. Just as people are always changing and never completely described by their names, so it is with mountains, from eons of upheaval and geologic alteration to the coyote tracks on the trail that change from this week to next.

Mountains always remind us of the big picture of life, the lure of beauty, and the mystery of the unknown. When we look at a panorama, we can barely take in every meadow or canyon at once. We can hardly contain the story of every softly worn trail, every small and large stream that contributes to the whole. Hidden from view one ridge over, a moose and her young calf may be browsing on willows downstream. Three ridges over, a small pack of wolves may be sniffing the air. Perhaps the urge to see it all, to know everything that is happening simultaneously, draws us to hike as deep and as far into the backcountry as we can. Like lovers exploring each other's bodies, we seek intimacy with the unknown. We want to know others as ourselves, to feel their pulse and contours.

When I explore a mountain, I am eager to smell all the damp canyons, finger the high plateau wildflowers, swim in each cold lake, and climb above the timberline to view the surrounding majesty. I move into the quiet air of high elevations and am immediately transported away from cities and concrete and cell phones into an older knowing far deeper and higher than my ordinary consciousness. In the mountains I gladly lose a sense of myself and eagerly give my ego over to the life forms of trees, streams, long open meadows, and steep, exciting trails. I am seldom ready to leave the heights on a day hike, and I turn for home only because my body tires or the sun does, and together we agree to call it a day.

Those who lived in mountain valleys before us, even as few as two hundred years ago, were without modern medicine and all the creature comforts we now so appreciate. By necessity, native peoples of the Rocky Mountain West were forced to have greater ties to the land; their cultures reinforced this connection, and continue to do so today. The chronicles of these Native Americans, both oral and written, speak of a deep respect for the mountains around them. They also had a healthy fear: that while they might find game for food, they could also be lost in a high country storm. They of course had no Gore-Tex clothing, no helicopter rescues, and no high-tech weather forecasts. What they did have was teachings about interdependence with the earth that inextricably linked them to the land. One of their many resources was a handed-down wisdom from their elders, including keen observations of animal instincts, teaching humans how to survive in nature. This included how and when to camp, hunt, and find shelter, food, and water.

To this day, many Native Americans sustain this close tie to the land. In addition, many non-Native people turn to various Indian tribes for help in understanding the human-earth relationship and for assistance in living in greater harmony with a nature on the brink of peril. A prime example of such cross-cultural sharing is the vision quest. While some Natives, who might be considered traditionalists, want non-Natives to only go to their own blood lineages for wisdom, others see and feel the urgency of sharing all they can for the good of the earth. For those Native Americans who believe that we are living in the time of the "Rainbow People," when all cultures must come together and share wisdom for the good of the planet and its inhabitants, vision quests are being taught as vital ceremonies for Indians and non-Indians alike.

Vision quests, often conducted in sacred lands in mountains to which tribal members have journeyed for years, begin with up to a year of preparation. This includes prayerful intention, paying attention to dreams and signs, and staying clear of altering substances. The purpose of such forethought is to help each person connect with "Spirit" on a deeper level and prepare to find wisdom, direction, and meaning. The actual quest involves spending a specified number of days alone without food and sometimes without water in the wilderness. The one who quests cries for a vision as a way of finding personal or, in contemporary language, professional direction, seeking a message from Great Spirit. Such messages will often come through some aspect of nature: an animal appearance, a weather pattern, or an actual spirit visitation. According to tribal custom, the message may be interpreted either by the one who quests or with the help of the elders. The entire tribe, or at least a small select group, prays continuously for the one on the quest. The power of this prayer is as crucial as the power of the quest itself.

Embedded in a vision quest is the core belief that nature contains all the answers we need. Non-native people today often do a less formal type of questing by spending time in nature to renew themselves. Those living near or in high mountain valleys sometimes consider themselves to be on a year-round type of questing, feeling inextricably connected to "their" mountains, not by ownership but by a sense of relationship. Like any good liaison, this human-to-place connection is nurtured by time spent listening, talking back and forth, falling silent, and basking in each other's presence.

If we are on a soul path of garnering inner wisdom, we intrinsically know when we need time to renew. Naturalist John Muir seemed to choose an almost lifelong vision quest. He lived for years in the wilderness in a state of ongoing awe, finding it to be "So fresh, so joyous, so immortal" (Edwin Way Teale, editor, *The Wilderness World of John Muir*, First Mariner Books: 2001). He described his cherished Sierra Mountains in early summer as "New life ... glorious, exuberant extravagance," and spoke of the "sublime wilderness." In my mind, he actually lived his vision in the wilderness itself. I am envious of his capabilities and choices, which brought him so many years of satisfaction and worshipful wonder.

My own briefer form of what I call a "white person's vision quest" arrived one year for me as an unexpected gift. The urge to renew my sense of life purpose and see if it was time to change careers had been intensifying for several months. One warm August day, as if in a trance, I simply realized I needed to go into the mountains for a few days. I cleared my schedule, called two friends and asked them to pray for me while I was gone, got in my car, and headed north. For safety, in case I was mauled by a bear or got lost, I told them I'd be somewhere on the west slopes of the Mission Mountains in northern Montana—only a several hundred-mile area if they needed to call out a search team. But the truth was, though I didn't want any harm to come to me, I wanted to be lost to them, to myself, and to my old life.

I left my ordinary reality, traveled the highways, and began to let something larger direct me up old dirt roads, steep inclines, and trails I'd never visited before. I let each day take me, camping in my car or some distance from it, journaling, reading, praying, laughing, moaning, keeping quiet. I concentrated on drawing close to the land rather than frightening myself, which meant that, one early evening, when two bears kept circling my camp, I deciphered my "teachings" and decided to drive down to a nearby motel. Sleeping in a bed while questing, I giggled to myself, was not all bad. In my younger years, I would have backpacked for days at a time. Now I courted easier creature comforts, at least for sleeping.

From early morning to late evening, as I tramped around the woods, other life forms continued to visit me. I had a bizarre encounter with a fetch of dragonflies, listened to tree wisdom, and met some young people at high elevation who thought that a middle-aged woman with an altered smile and uncombed hair who was "questing" was totally eccentric and "very cool." Three days' worth of experience later, I realized the unplanned results: a deeper knowing of how the earth must be preserved, as well as confirmation of the soulful work I was doing with other humans. I'd found my center for my current life and reaffirmed a deeper sense of serenity and soul. Having given myself freedom to change career tracks—even my entire life—I emerged with assurance that all that needed changing was my deepening relationship with myself and God. With such intimacy renewed, I breathed in the undisturbed mountain air around me, bid farewell to the small lakes and streams I'd meditated beside, and returned home packed with more life than my body or my Jeep could hold.

We all perform a type of vision quest each time we go consciously alone into the vastness of nature and tune in to the symphony of sounds, sights, and impressions around us. We can take in the sounds with ears open to hear new messages and our eyes open to see new visions, while an invisible essence deposits itself into our hearts. In the heart of the mountains, everything foggy becomes clear and everything fine becomes possible.

Specific mountain ranges appeal to certain individuals. My own favorites are the mountains that ring the Gallatin Valley of southwest Montana, where I have lived for over twenty years. I must tell you again their names because, like friends, they deserve proper attention. They are the approachable Bridger Mountains to the east, the magic Tobacco Roots to the west, and the dramatic Spanish Peaks to the south that herald the Gallatin Range and extend down the canyon to Big Sky and on into Yellowstone Park. Behind the Bridgers, beyond the brief Bangtail Mountains, to the east of our valley and more foreboding but also more exciting, are the Crazy Mountains, where hypothermia is as common as nightfall. I lived in the Crazy Mountains for a year in a log cabin warmed only by a small wood-burning stove, and I can attest to the crazy-making storms.

I blush with self-consciousness to reveal that the reason I love these particular mountain ranges so much is because I imagine that eons ago I had something to do with their formation. Maybe I was a beam of light who lovingly watched or helped with their creation, or an energy form that assisted as their peaks and valleys uplifted and settled. Regardless, in this life I have fallen in love with these ranges, an emotion as strong as love for another human. I feel the urge to check up on each of them both summer and fall, following my favorite trails and looking for evidence of health or disease. Thankfully, because of the efforts of many local and national preservation groups, these mountains and their entire ecosystems continue to be fought for and protected. I pray and sing to these human helpers and to the mountains themselves. Native wisdom and my own remind me that all life forms are my blood relatives, my elders, my nieces and nephews, and all are to be acknowledged.

Though the flatlands of the Midwest and the rolling hills of the South have their own mystique, mountains maintain, for me, a more captivating mystery. Because their varied heights hide secrets, mountains will, like life, offer ways of being surprised by the unknown. Mountains will always offer sustenance to those who seek it. Although Western religion at times seems to see nature as competitive with God, claiming worship of nature as pagan and therefore sinful, the French translation of pagan is "country dweller who lives close to God." The book of Psalms in the Bible itself speaks of the impulse to "lift up mine eyes unto the hills, from whence cometh my strength." Surely God dwells there. Eastern religions have made the world's highest mountains their monasteries and temples for centuries. Our spiritual yearning to get close to the Creator in the mountains is a valuable part of our earth experience. Some people cannot live anywhere but the mountains—mountains they can climb into as though curling up in the lap of God. Though all things change in any given lifetime, mountains endure. They refer us to the larger landscape of life and offer a steady reminder of the bigger picture, helping us place the small stories of our lives against the backdrop of the vastness of all creation. Mountains invite us to their mystery, welcoming us with canyoned calls and echoes. Listen. Are they calling you?

5

The Good Earth

The thoughts of the earth are my thoughts ... the voice of the earth is my voice ... All that belongs to the earth belongs to me ... It is lovely indeed.

—from "Song of the Earth Spirit," Navajo origin legend

The earth literally supports us. Gravity provides just the right pull to keep our feet grounded even as our spirits lift upward to the heavens. It also has the incredible capacity to constantly delight us with its attributes while reminding us of our limitations. We stand in awe of a grove of sequoias, unable to leap even a fraction of their height. In cities, we may live in high-rises on suspended concrete floors, but we must have grounding for our feet below us.

I love to move my body into almost any posture imaginable to make contact with the earth. Rolling, walking, running, skipping, and rocking all connect me to the soil and grass. Lying on the earth face down is a wonderful way to access my playful inner child and to reconnect with the marvel of the ground. In the right season, I can find an open meadow, a streamside bank, or a soft-needled base of an old fir tree and stretch out. I let my whole body make full contact with the earth. I feel my own pulse and body rhythm begin to adjust to what is below me. Suddenly I notice the ants, the grasses, the twigs, and the sureness of each aspect of my immediate world. Now there is no need for confusion, no holding of breath, no pulling away from anything. Here the earth teaches me to not pull away from myself. The earth has not abandoned itself because there is nowhere else for it to go, nowhere else to be, nothing else for it to do. The same, in this moment, is true for me. This is where my breath deepens, and this is how my soul connects.

Some people carry what healers and therapists call "earth energy." These people tend to be salt-of-the earth types: safe, comforting, warm, solid, and reliable as the earth itself. Earth people have deep connections with life and like being close to the ground. These same people, however, can suffer from depression, since having too much earth in their personalities can tap their energy and cause them to forget the buoyancy of spirit. People with "sky energy," on the other hand, are full of light, ideology, philosophy, and spirituality. They are imbued with inspiration, but may be deemed "spacey" and forget or choose not to take care of life's practical demands. Sky people need earth to ground them and help them be connected, efficient, and rooted in the everyday tasks of living. The earth helps both types. It offers the reassurance of home to those who are already rooted and draws those who are too ethereal back to the earth plane and the embodiment of their lives. I am primarily "earth." I move slowly, tend to carry "mother energy," and can also be depressed, especially in winter, when light is low and time outdoors scarce.

Earth teaches us many useful concepts. Through its example, we see the change of each season; we know that all life forms are born, grow, and die. We are taught how death feeds every other living thing in the food cycle. Awakening to the fact that all life has its own season can be temporarily overwhelming until we recognize the universal truth that earth offers: life feeds other life. We also learn how the earth continues to go through its cycles, even when a valued person or animal has passed on. We who are still alive will grieve, but we will eventually go through that final transition ourselves. We will rest in the good earth then, or our ashes may. Meanwhile, the solidity of earth offers us a stable home.

All earth asks of us in return for its available wisdom and support of ecospheres is that we not overuse its resources. With world population growth, our species has pushed that natural balance over the limit. We need to encourage sane, earth-healthy reproductive choices so that we continue to have open space, clean dirt, and lots of mud to mess around with.

Many people are birthing a new consciousness about the earth and our relationship to it. Although their numbers may still be a small percentage of the world's people, these consciousness groups and individuals are gathering in healing circles, holding conferences, and taking action of necessity, spurred by the agony and ecstasy of awakening to the earth's needs. Jacquelyn Small's insightful book *Awakening in Time* describes a few steps to help us achieve this kind of earth awareness. She and others in her field urge us to:

* Awaken to our soul's evolution;

* Take concrete action to actualize it; and

* Deepen our connection with the Divine in preservation and conservation.

Bill Plotkin, through his seminal work *Soulcraft,* reminds us that earth provides a personal testing ground for our soulful and physical development and that we can learn from stretching our sense of limitation as well as from limitation itself. His program in southwest Colorado invites seekers into rites of passage through the earth's majesty and challenges.

Even with all the contemporary horrors of pollution and toxic soils, the earth still contains so much beauty. As we take time to physically inundate ourselves with its enveloping fields and backcountry quiet, the earth lovingly carves trails back to us that create new passages in the untraveled places of our souls. The delight of taking the time to be conscious of personal experience with the earth renews body, mind, and spirit. In the process of doing so, it may not be so much that *we* discover as that *we are* discovered, truly known by the earth itself, our home and much-needed source of nurturing and solidity in our lives.

6

The Standing People

Walking, I can almost hear the redwoods beating ...
Be still, they say. Watch and listen. You are the result of the love of thousands.

—Linda Hogan, Chickasaw poet

How fabulous that we are "the result of the love of thousands"—thousands of seedlings, thousands of appreciative human spirits, thousands of beetles and birds and grains of soil all providing the environment in which to grow.

Trees have long been referred to by many Native American tribes as "the Standing People." The reverence these tribes, as well as Celtic descendants of Northern Europe, give to trees is clear: trees, like humans, have the right to place, to attention, and to figure strongly in tribal wisdom. To walk with an attentive ear into a grove of trees is to hear your own belonging. The essence absorbed may be that of a story, an impression, or a vision that encourages the listener in personal or communal life. Native peoples in all countries know that if you suspend doubt and allow trees to talk to you, and believe what you hear, your life will be changed—and blessed. Author David Abrams explains, through his creative book *The Spell of the Sensuous,* that we have to "shed the accepted perceptual logic [and] to enter into relation with other species ... alter the common organization of [our] senses." I have found this to be abundantly true.

Not long ago, I had the great pleasure of finding myself in a grove of Linden trees on Innisfallen Island in the middle of Lake Killarney in Ireland. Oddly, I find an energetic earth connection between Ireland and Montana, which I know will reveal itself to me someday. But for this day, on that small emerald island, I had just snuck away from a week-long international conference I'd been attending on eco-psychology. It was a fascinating gathering, but too overwhelming for my energies to take in all at once. I instinctively headed for the little island and was carried over to it by a boatman who sang old Irish songs quietly under his breath as the motor churned us to our destination. Come back in time and experience it with me.

As the fisherman's small tour boat sputters toward the waiting island, I am lulled into a kind of reverie from some past, some calling I cannot quite hear. But it is pleasant, so I give over to the rhythm of roll and the approaching land. As we arrive on the island, the other tourists disembark and follow the boatman, who begins to lilt about the abbey ruins, the kings and queens who stayed here, the time before Saint Patrick. I slip away from the group to a far corner of the abbey ruins and curl up on a large, flat stone. Before I know it, I am half-asleep yet coming alive to an older consciousness. I vaguely hear the group approaching and our guide's chuckle to the group. "Oh," he says, motioning toward me, "I see she's found her Queenship. This is where the royalty used to stay. I'll call for her highness when we're ready to depart." He leans closer to me as the others are milling by. "You can stay here all day," he half whispers. "But my last departure will be an hour before sunset. If you miss it, you'll have to stay overnight. Is that shawl enough to keep you warm?"

I offer a groggy smile and nod at him. I'm relieved as they all take their leave to other parts of the abbey. I am already melting away to some other time. As their voices fade, however, I feel suddenly refreshed, as though from a long nap. I sit up and glance around at the small mile-long expanse of island. I am drawn to rise and walk along the barely worn trail that circles this tiny piece of land surrounded by tranquil waters.

My steps begin to feel like someone else's, as though I'm walking back in history. Yet I am not as concerned with my own identity as with the energy of singing birds, each bush, and each tree I pass by. Around the northwest corner, somewhere between memory and the elders, a grove of beech trees greets me with sudden interest. Immediately transformed, I stand up straight in the grove, wanting to mimic the trees' own trunks, and throw my arms wide, forever trying to look like one of them. I am keen to listen. Voices, familiar to each other, begin to talk to me; I can actually hear them assuring they have seen "the woman of the trees." I smile in delight at having been recognized by distant relatives and am honored by their murmured and hushed greetings.

Many notes at once converge to form a hum I might never hear again, the history of these worlds, and origins, and beyond. All are proffered in layered offerings coming fast to my altered ears. Time passes as with the company of old familiar friends while I listen to their stories of eons of time and gaze at their branches dipping with the soft breezes from the lake. At some point I climb onto a large round stone, close to the shore yet hidden in the vast canopy of this ancient stand, and open my journal to try to record the vastness of the impressions they are imparting. Yet soon I close my journal and just move into beingness with the grove itself.

The sun is low in the sky when a boat horn startles me, bellowing from the far side of the island. I groan, leaning in toward my suddenly fast-fading experience. In response to my lapsed attention, the beech trees seem to settle back into their trunks, looking more like pictures in a book again, and my mouth falls open to the wonder of the blessing I've just received. I realize I'll be returning with the last boat of the day after all. I've gotten what I came to receive. Bowing good-bye and running fast on the matted path to the old cloister and boat dock, I find the boatman loading passengers back in his craft. He smiles up at my breathless countenance and nods, eyes gleaming.

"Now, ladies and gentlemen," he croons softly, looking around at his seated audience, "Don'tcha know, if you but stand still here long enough, you could put a hand through the other side." He nods again at me. The other passengers look blank, but he knows, and so do I. The island becomes me, and I am hardly aware I am a human body being transported back to the mainland. Yet the trilling of the birds on Innisfallen recedes with the lapping of oar over oar until shore at last claims us in the late afternoon light.

I return to the conference carrying the essence of the grove and the fast-fading knowledge it had so generously shared with me. Under the large meeting tent, the director and the thematic presenter both look at me, and the presenter says, in a kind of wonder, "You are so earthy, like a walking tree. Would you like to hold the element of earth for us tonight in our ceremony?" I agree, and beam, and move in a stately fashion back to my grove of humans.

No matter where in the world I've traveled, I have found trees to possess unique characteristics. Some trees are regal and seem to offer an ancient wisdom and vast creativity; others are lighter and more playful, perhaps enlivening sensuality or sexuality. If we ask, and it allows, we may also be able to shamanically enter a tree itself. We simply request permission and then allow ourselves to believe what happens: feel the sap running in our veins, feel the rootedness and the silent wisdom learned from standing so still and observing for so long. We may experience sensory, 'felt' perception, thought forms, or emotions. Or it may simply be an experience of stilling the self to rebalance body-mind-spirit.

We may not always hear all that goes on in nature, because the wide range of information may be too great for typically tuned-out senses. We need to take time to allow increasing sensitivity toward the life in everything around us. When we remember that all life originates in a spirit of love and tenderness, we will be tender with ourselves and trust that we will "awaken in time," a phrase metaphysical teacher Jacquelyn Small uses to describe our call to greater consciousness. Awakening in time, in my cosmology, means to become conscious of the urgency of our ultimate goals as evolving humans by living as nature would teach us. It hearkens back to esoteric teachings and pulls us forward to catch up with the insistent calls of contemporary visionaries. It asks us to connect vast Spirit with earthly Soul, and in doing so to rebalance ourselves individually and globally. It asks us to not destroy the planet on which we live. It embodies an understanding of the sentience of all things, including trees and the stories they tell.

The messages of trees can be heard everywhere, whether they grow in cities or the country, in flatlands or mountains. Each one has something important to impart. If you want to receive, trust the creative process to lead you into previously unknown forms of understanding. Let your body release into a given tree or grove of trees and believe it as it offers to take you on an inner journey. Find out from it what you need to know and what you need to do. Then do the tough work of integrating this knowledge into the practicalities of everyday life. That is something they generally can't do for you; it is up to you to find out how to use the wisdom they've imparted. Go even further and help to preserve our Standing People. When you work to protect trees, you'll discover even more about them.

If we can return to seeing trees as sentient beings and not primarily as fuel, paper products, and home-building sources, we can restore their rightful place on earth. If we are Western Caucasians, we will release our arrogance about our "manifest destiny," ceasing to use nature and other people for our own greed. If we are part of developing countries, we will hold fiercely to finding ways to preserve nature while providing economic sustenance.

The Standing People have a wisdom that we humans may never completely intuit. I once heard a respected native elder say that each tree species has completed its particular evolution and is waiting for humans to wake up and hear its stories so we can all evolve to a better world. Trees may be able to help us awaken, if we allow ourselves to listen. Perhaps we can learn to treat them with the same love and tenderness that Native Americans and other indigenous cultures have given them for centuries. As a poem I have written attempts to suggest, trees are marvelous, sentient beings.

The Standing People

Do you know about the ancient trees
The way their graying lower branches pull out, brittle and sure?
How roots weave in and out of needled earth
How long green arms commune with the sky?
They share secrets we may hear if we are still long enough
While sap runs old down red-barked grooves of passage.
We can talk about the deep world of charred knowing
Root-solid, reaching, gathered ...
How we have lost the thread of their quiet conversation
How when we cut their ancient wisdom
Our own memory began to decay.
Worn now in spirit, we hesitate—
Peer into the vanishing wild—
And wonder if it can save us from ourselves.
Move close to trees and be still, wherever you find them.
Then the Standing People will assume their full height
Running courage through our veins faster than we can
Tap sap from theirs,
Rooting us to a life in one accord.

7
The Stone People

In a certain stone, I see all the faces of my patient, undone self.
—Anon

North of Bozeman, Montana, sits a unique 160-acre property owned by a rancher friend. There, thousands of mossy rocks have slid and landed as if still planning to go somewhere. These rocks have much to say. If you were to walk quietly up the slopes of this pristine area, you would begin to hear their excited conversations. I have spent hours walking through their tumbled company and sitting on their larger relatives, soaking up the environment and growing still in myself. As I quiet my mental chatter, I begin to hear the sounds they are always in the middle of making. Rocks converse in the way that only rocks know how to do. Sometimes the cacophony grows so strong I blurt out "Wait! One at a time, please!"

Indigenous societies have always listened to rocks. "The Stone People," as many tribes call them, have wise voices. They hold a special kind of condensed knowledge. Stones are particularly good at being present while holding generations of history. I certainly project my own needs and desires onto the Stone People, but I also hear their own responses—when I am empty enough to listen. I trust that you too will hear what you need to hear, according to your soul path. One person's soul may be focused on finding truth; another may keen after relationships. One desires personal success; another seeks to be spiritually astute. The Stone People will guide you in whatever you need to know, which may be different from what you thought! They may well talk about the condition of the world and their geographic place in particular. It may help to have a journal or even a portable recorder handy to record impressions; I find that if I don't, the messages fade from consciousness too fast, and all I am left with is awe from remembering that they 'said' something amazing. But my body remembers. I know this because of the great peace I feel afterwards.

What you actually hear may be a blend of your own ideas and the true presence of another sentient form. However, the more often and keenly you listen to the Stone People, the less of your own ego you will hear. Ego is projection's driving force. When I am full of myself, I extend my own views to all those around me and am only able to make sense of the world as I see it. The philosopher George Santayana, in a speech given at the University of California campus in Berkeley in 1911, criticized Western materialism and condemned the idea that humans were the center of the universe. Santayana suggested close, personal contact with nature as the antidote to such personally driven thoughts. He pointed to American writers such as Henry David Thoreau and Walt Whitman as examples of those who developed a more democratic and even objective view of nature and the cosmos. He was asking us to listen to the "sacred other" in nature to learn a new way of knowing, far beyond our normal grasp of things. We relearn to delight and thrill to the Great Mystery through personal experience.

I am picking my way through my friend's rock-laden property while my ankles complain and threaten to collapse if I don't take more care. As always, I greet the rocks in a kind of hush, full of excitement, but they seem to have no ego-personality. They are personal yet matter-of-fact. I have the impression that some of the Stone People I am tromping over want their privacy. Others are more gregarious. The delight for me is in discerning the differences and still saying yes to every experience, having learned over time that nature, or my soul, or God will offer only the messages I am ready to hear. The Stone People seem to have different histories and functions. When I stand or sit still and listen to them, I hear its stories about what it is like for him or her to have landed where they have, what the years of erosion, weather, and human interference have done to them. In being close to and touching their smooth surfaces, I also begin to remember my own deep hopes and wishes, as well as fond memories. I have found the Stone People to also be prophets and seers, able to foretell what I might require to live life in greater freedom. They reveal more each time I return, helping me open my heart and mind to the great story of creation itself.

Stones serve ceremonial functions for us in our everyday human lives more than we tend to realize. A simple ring of stones around a campfire creates a type of container that holds both literal and metaphorical significance. Literally, it holds the heat so the participants can benefit from warmth without getting burned by fire. A circle of stones symbolically and esoterically hearkens back to the "ring without end," the circle being the healing shape of completion for the human psyche. A ring of campfire stones also encourages us to circle around it and to face each other in a commonality and equality, often by telling stories or singing. Whether sacred or irreverent, the experience later evokes memories of camp nights.

Stones play major roles in landscaped residential areas. A stone walkway in my own yard defines a path of beauty. I have to admit I have paid more than I would have imagined for several unique lichen-strewn boulders that I have had placed around my property. Each of these boulders became instant friends from the moment I saw, touched, and sat on their cold, bumpy bodies. Some instant knowing in my gut said, "Yes, we'll have many good conversations down the way," and before I knew it, my credit card came out, and the boulders followed me home.

I have also settled for smaller boulders, those small, smoothed handheld stones sold in gift stores with engraved words of encouragement carved on them—words like "vision," "peace," or "forgiveness." Some are carved with replicas of ancient petroglyphs or animal imprints. And I, like many, also have a prized bevy of specially shaped stones collected from streambeds, oceans, and special hikes. Each one claims its place as a souvenir of a particular day.

Rocks are embedded in our patterns of speech. We refer to the solidity or appeal of rocks, as in "solid as a rock" and "a piece of the rock" and "a rolling stone gathers no moss." They are also the physical emblems for marking the directions of east, south, west, and north in Native American medicine wheels. The types of stones chosen for these healing circles are very important; the choices are sacred, since the stones are considered to have sacred functions.

You may want to find or return to a place where you can meet with the Stone People. It may be a rock outcropping full of moss, lichen, and trickling water. It may be a desert boulder or cave. It may be a volcanic outpouring or a simple few gathered by a stream. They may help you, as they've helped me, to understand life's purpose by "doing your being" as well as "being your doing." They are so sure and certain. A sense of the meaning of life may come to you in a sudden almost unbelievable *ping!* "Oh, but that's so easy!" you may exclaim, or, "I've known and done this all my life!" The apparent simplicity is part of the gift.

Recognizing your possible life purpose is only the start. Your life's colors, textures, and designs develop naturally and effortlessly as you learn to love your existence. The Stone People can remind you of the innocence and easy beliefs of your child self; then, if you are willing, you can integrate this ancient knowledge into your adult capabilities and find better ways of living day-to-day.

When I need this type of earth medicine, I connect with the rough texture and musty smells of the Stone People in their natural environment; their nearness excites my senses. My nose inhales old and undisturbed scents. My hands softly touch their green, lichen-covered bodies, and if they seem agreeable to it, I turn them over for inspection, always being sure to place them back as they were. Some are overgrown with orange and yellow. All carry a story: how the colors formed over time on their backs, how the north shade always protects them, how it is that they weather in their environments, how even their breaking open is part of their natural response to the great pressures of living. Their cool temperatures calm their visitors' summer sweats, and the human heart slows to match their hidden pulse.

You can make arrangements to travel anytime that weather and your schedule allows to visit the Stone People. Or you can renew old acquaintance with special mementos you've gathered and taken home over the years as souvenirs of special places. Hold them to your ear, your mouth, and your heart. They wait for you; they've been waiting for centuries.

8

The Air We Breathe

Breath is life; life is breath. Breathe. What else do you need to do?

—Sufi saying

When was the last time you took in a deep breath of fresh mountain air, filling your lungs with the scents of pine and willows and the good earth? Research claims that many species of trees carry natural immunity boosters in the scents emanating from leaves and bark. Some fortunate souls breathe in such unpolluted air daily. Ironically, the higher the elevation, the thinner the air—there are fewer oxygen molecules at altitude. Breathing pure mountain air means breathing less of what we need. Nevertheless, isn't high, fresh air preferable to that of lower elevations, polluted cities, and surrounding communities?

A young woman I know just returned from Bangkok, Thailand, where she worked with a team of city managers to consider the use of ethanol for motorbikes rather than the current non-emission-controlled petrol. The issue is a complicated one, since ethanol cuts carbon and other pollutants but has a larger impact on the ozone layer. Do they choose less pollution for the present but more danger from a decreased layer of ozone, which keeps out the sun's damaging ultraviolet rays, in the future? As we recognize that all humans breathe the same air on the same globe, we realize that the plight of Thailand is the plight of the world.

Breathing in air is easier to want to do in a less polluted area. Your body will benefit from breathing in good air deeply on a regular basis. Deep breaths oxygenate your cells, combating a host of physical maladies, from high blood pressure to chronic muscle aches. Deep breaths into the abdomen refresh and rejuvenate cells. Many of us tend to take shallow breaths, pulling air only into the upper chest. Look at people in a crowd or walking by, and you will see how they hold their breath. Women often do not belly breathe, since as girls we were taught to hold our tummies in. Men often breathe into their upper backs or upper stomachs, being "strong and upright" and holding tension around their midriffs. You will notice that many people have a deadness in their hips, genital areas, and limbs. Yet when you see people who could be described as "natural" or "sensual," they are most likely breathing fully throughout their whole body and, as a result, move freely. The relaxation and aliveness you feel when you practice full-body breathing will help you remember to breathe deeply more often.

For centuries, sages have taught many forms of rejuvenating breath. I teach a contemporary form of Breathwork based on some of these ancient practices. I tell people who do Breathwork that they are very courageous. None of us know what psychological material will surface as a result of deep and continuous breathing. That is why it is important to do this work with a well-trained therapist who knows how to help open the psyche while providing a safe container for the contents. It connects you with the Divine and deepens your soul life. It enhances the very air you need. What's not to love?

Today a September breeze ruffles the aspen leaves surrounding the porch of a log-framed restaurant where I am sitting outside having dinner. I am breathing effortlessly, but I take a deeper breath when the breeze touches me. In this protected mountain retreat, ensconced at the edge of a quiet meadow, the sound of the approaching wind through the trees excites my child-mind. What shuttles along so confidently with that sighing wind? Stories, warnings, and reminders come to me. I can hear the wind approaching dramatically as it builds and cascades through miles of dense forest before it actually arrives at the open hillside cleared for cabins and lawns and a stable of horses. It lifts the horses' manes capriciously, yet they turn their ears only slightly in acknowledgment, while I am full of the unsettled moment. They are so much more accustomed to the wild and unexpected than am I! The wind careens past a large mountain peak, and then it is gone. Afterward, in the lull of its absence, a stale quiet ensues, and the flies of late summer return, buzzing frantically at my table as if they know that approaching fall weather marks their end. Suddenly, the wind again casts ribbons down into the meadow, flickering leaves and scattering sunshine into patterns. The flies head for shelter, and I attempt to remember to breathe through my amazement, letting the wind cavort through my now-chilled arms and chest.

The next time you find yourself in a wind of any capacity, whether a welcome breeze or stormy gale, you may remember to breathe deep the gathering air. Even if you don't have a wind to inspire you, you can always pull air deep to your belly and mentally direct it into all your stagnant places. Breathe out and release all you were holding in, all you don't need, all that makes you ill. Breathe in once again, taking in all the fullness that life offers. Expand your courage to live. Then release it and, with it, all that is old and stale. Repeat that cycle a few times again. Your life force of breath is your own breeze. On a windy day, you can whisper this mantra over and over until it becomes your own: "This is how I know myself: by how the breeze enchants me."

9

Mysteries of the Deep

We call upon the waters that rim the earth, horizon to horizon ... Teach us, and show us the Way.
—Chinook invocation

Our oceans contain entire worlds within themselves. In my younger years, while I was swimming over coral reefs in Hawaii, a female whale swam close. In my excitement I opened my mouth to exclaim and of course gulped sea water. I was completely at home in her massive presence. She could do anything personal to me, and I wouldn't take it personally. It would actually be an honor. As I saw her eyes fix on mine, she communicated depths of sentient knowledge in an instant. I was so thrilled that later I forgot what she "said." It was a kind of visitation by God.

The fascinating wisdom of oceans, with such astounding variety of shapes, colors, and sizes of fish, corals, and mystery, are the clearest signs of a Creator I can imagine. Many people are content to travel to an ocean and perhaps wade at the shore without feeling the need to be completely immersed in it. However, some of us have to swim forth, braving jellyfish and possible sharks to feel the free wildness of a large expanse of water. While swimming in the ocean depths, I have heard humpback whales sing to each other underwater. In the Galapagos Islands off Ecuador, I have shared the water with hammerhead sharks—albeit inadvertently. Our snorkeling guide had tapped the fins of our vulnerable group to alert us that the hammerheads were approaching quite quickly. A school of one hundred of them were soon swimming a mere twenty feet below us. I doubt any of us blinked while they leisurely swam by. Our guide had promised that there had never been a shark attack in the entire island chain. "The reason," he added casually, "is that there are so many recognizable fish in such plentiful supply that they don't need humans." *This was a comfort?* I wondered. When he spotted a white shark up ahead, however, he quickly herded us back to the boat. "Better safe than sorry," he added, a bit pale. We only glimpsed the large, white body breaking the surface of the ocean briefly, and turned our fins in quick retreat. The excitement surged through me long after the quick scramble up the boat's welcoming ladder.

Whenever I return to land after any sea adventure, I am left with a lingering appreciation for the vast mystery of ocean life that lives perfectly without care for me or any other two-legged creatures. I marvel that while I am eating a meal on land, in the ocean next to me the fish are busy and content eating algae or each other. Each being is one small link in a complete and long-acknowledged food chain. I also think of how human thoughtlessness has polluted their world of the sea, impacting fish, mammals, and birds, even destroying entire species. The anchored as well as self-propelled creatures of the oceans remind us that we must not destroy their world, even though we do not often see deeply into it.

Freshwater lakes contain their own mysteries. One of my favorite places is Lake Tahoe, legendary and historic home of the Washoe and Paiute Indians. Stretched along the California-Nevada border, Tahoe is one of those lakes that seems especially blessed, in spite of roads and overcrowding. When I swim into its cold, blue-green waters, I can feel the lake's sacred beauty. I don't know why certain lakes seem so sentient to some of us while others seem more ordinary. Perhaps, like most mysteries, part of the beauty is in not knowing; it is what is invisible that attracts us. Tahoe holds this attractive mystery for many of its admirers, myself included. Like many sacred places that are endowed by a special sense of grace, it has its own undisturbed essence. Its depth and range of color from deep blue to emerald green creates visual pleasure and an underwater visibility of eighty feet. Immersing oneself in the water's beauty inspires trust and relaxation. It helps our finite bodies of watery human emotion find their place in a larger body. The last time I vacationed there, I swam directly toward the center of the lake (as I usually do), foolishly braving motor boats and ignoring caution because of the magnetic pull that harnesses me. Lately I had been feeling disconnected from myself and others, my spirit loose in the wind, my body not even able to feel the cold water numbing my skin. As I continued to swim, however, I could feel myself traveling toward the welcome arms of the cold mother who dwells, in my imagination (and I hope in reality), in the middle of that lake. She *is* the Lady of the Lake, in real and palpable form, extending her wet heart into and through my body, if only I open myself enough for her blessings. Paddling out farther, I "heard" with my inner ear a story about how the Divine Feminine is always available and waiting for us, no matter how long we have been away or how we have strayed from her kindnesses. I soaked up her message, my body thirsty for the renewed sense of belonging that was bestowed upon me.

Water holds a unique capacity to heal. If you start to feel lost in the waters of your own emotion, why not employ a homeopathic tonic? You can go to a lake or ocean, which will amplify, recognize, and settle out your emotional state through its own larger body of emotion. Your unconscious can communicate with you more easily when you immerse yourself in the larger, deeper unconscious of a clear lake. The homeopathic remedy is to stand in water, sit in water, swim above and underwater, living in and touching water so that it can begin to pull order from your chaos, talk to you, rebalance you, and teach you what you need to know. The more you love it, the more it loves you back.

For those who doubt, quantum physics is now proving that water absorbs not only physical substances like toxins; it also absorbs human thought! The fascinating work of Dr. Emoto (author of *Messages from Water* and whose work appeared in the movie *What the Bleep?*) has shown that water absorbs energy vibrations. He has photographed water crystals that have been given loving words and cruel ones. The crystals influenced by the loving words are well formed, bright, and beautiful. The ones exposed to negative words are blurry, dull, and look toxic. Likewise, music and prayerful intention have also been shown to affect water. What an amazing carrier it is.

Recently a colleague and I gave a presentation on the sentience of water at a conference on consciousness. We had two identical jars of water: one that we had blessed and one that we hadn't. We asked the participants to taste each sample and determine which was the blessed water. In other tests like this, the average member of the public enjoys about 60 percent accuracy, while children score 90 percent accuracy. This conscious group we were working with scored 90 percent accuracy also, like the children. Does consciousness help return us to our more natural state, similar to that which we knew as youngsters?

Since this research is establishing water's reflection of positive emotions, it makes sense to both bless and be blessed by large bodies of water, particularly ones you love. I enjoy swimming, so when my own emotions are strong, I immerse myself in a lake, ocean, or wide stream, lolling in waves or stillness and feeling the larger fluidity around me. I often try to position myself upright in deep water with arms open wide, leaning my head back in a position of what I call "active surrender." Because I am in a vertical position, I am active, not cowed in a victim stance, and because my arms are thrown wide, I am surrendering to a higher way, intentionally aligning myself with a greater wisdom.

I also consciously connect my emotional body to the outer activity of swimming. While swimming, I let myself either experience the metaphor of gliding effortlessly through challenges, or I just fully participate in my current emotional state, accepting however I feel. It does not take long before the waters identify, calm, and rebalance my feelings. My own fluid awareness is activated through the greater body of water. Homeopathically, I bring my emotional state to the same larger emotion, as carried by water.

I let it hold my small story in the vastness of its larger one.

Once this alchemical process has completed itself, which never takes long, I begin to absorb and kinesthetically feel the positive effects of an ordered psyche. This has been especially helpful when visiting at a lake with family and all the attendant emotions and unfinished, unexpressed business we all tend to have with one another. If I take my hurt, or anger, or confusion right into the cold waters of my sentient lake, I soon find myself soothed and rebalanced. And I usually receive teachings about my part in any encounter I've had with a family member. This helps me return to my human tribe with much more wisdom.

Whether you are a natural water lover or not, water can be an excellent treatment for overwhelming, unidentified, or stuck emotions. Immersing ourselves in a larger body connects us to the greater whole and helps uncover a greater acceptance of all that is watery by nature. Plunging into a salty ocean or a large, clear lake settles our psyches and organizes our small lives while connecting us to the big life of the planet. Through conscious and active choice, we are healed and realigned through the mysteries and secret powers of the deep.

10
River Songs

You cannot step twice into the same stream, for fresh waters are ever flowing upon you.
—Heraclitus

I am fortunate to live in a mountainous environment where many of our streams are relatively toxin-free. On summer days, I travel to the high mountain rivers to spend peaceful hours. I seem to need their sustenance in order to return to the transformative inner work I facilitate for myself and for others.

I am wandering along a barely defined trail by the lovely Gallatin River, which flows for miles through my hometown of Bozeman and caprices through the upscale Big Sky ski development oblivious of the fact that the multimillion dollar homes are all trying to imitate what it already exudes: power, beauty, renewal, cleanliness, refreshment. Mountains flank the sides of this large-bouldered river, which in dark moments has seen fatal rafting and kayaking accidents, and in lighter times has heard the delighted squeals of tourists during the more successful water trips. No one is on the water near me now, however, as I carefully pick my way through the light-green sage and long-leafed willows along the river's edge, watching for gopher or snake holes as I pad along. The water jumps and swirls in eddies like it is telling its own private jokes. I laugh, pretending I am privy to the humor.

When I fall silent, I become more pensive. I wonder why I need to come to rivers to release tension and difficulty. Today I am full of too many client stories of horrific abuses, tired of dealing with my own family stressors, and just tired of work. This is when my inner critic has a field day. "You shouldn't have to rely on nature," it chides me. "You're weak and not enough. That's why you have to do this."

Like an abused child myself, I merely nod, my chin lowering toward the waves and swirls near my feet. With a sigh, I sink down to the rocky earth. My eyes glaze while my feet find their way into the edge of the bracing flow, and I allow the water to swirl around them like children hugging a weary parent. In that moment, I immediately belong. Critical thoughts are swept downstream, and I once again know who I am. I am a child of the universe. I fit. I should be here. "Here" meaning I belong to my life on earth. I am not wrong or evil or unforgivable. I do not have to hold onto anything negative like that. I don't even have to hold on to how loved I know I am—by God, by others, by nature itself. The sounds of the river turn to primordial, celestial music rushing through my brain, washing out all other noise, and I simply become it— the wet, flowing, sloshing, gurgling mess of clarity and opposites all colliding and melting and mixing and alchemizing into pure joyous nonspecific neutrality.

Now I look around me. Now I can consider a human thought again, as in, *What if a moose comes down here for a drink?* I hope that one will. What a fun surprise. I think if one came upon me suddenly it wouldn't attack; I think it would recognize its own mistake and, even if startled, deftly pick up those long front legs and wheel away, trotting down that trail a bit, where it would look back at me once again, blow out its nostrils, and lower that long, rounded muzzle into the stream. That is what I imagine, and for today, that is where the experience stays. But it feels as real as though it actually happened, and I laugh with the thrill of it. "Virtual reality," as it is called by quantum physicists. I'll take it any way I can get it.

Rivers teach me how to move through abandonment to belonging through their always changing yet always similar landscape. Sometimes

I hide feelings of abandonment from others, and even myself, holing up in a stagnant, private pond where no one can find me. But every time I'm willing to surrender and release my angst to the flow of a fast-moving river or meandering stream, I re-enter the flow of life. When any of us feel abandoned, we can let go into the river and feel the truth of being lost to the ferocity of the river's relentless force. We can then release ourselves out of this vortex and once again flow in freedom through life, bouncing and cascading along.

Our sense of belonging ironically re-engages when we understand the flow of loss and renewal. When we feel abandoned, the river teaches us that everything changes, and we'd better not try to hold too fast to anything, because it will be swept downstream. It becomes so much easier to flow with the river than to endlessly paddle upstream. The more we get comfortable with allowing a sense greater than ourselves to carry us downstream, the easier life becomes. A sense of belonging ensues, a belonging even to being lost. Once recognized, this in turn loops back to our sense of belonging by being found. Rivers are never lost to themselves.

The relentless flow of the river, while establishing the temporal nature of our life plans, also metaphorically reveals how to die and be no more while still reappearing in new forms. It is not an intellectual exercise; it is a corporeal experience. It is intimate and direct, searching and revealing. Very encouraging, these rivers we thought were only pretty to look at, to fish from, or to harness. Of course, these are the secrets many dedicated fishermen and fisherwomen know, whether or not they have put it into words. The understanding is there. They know the river; they *are* the river. Avid fishermen will tell you that being on a river is second to none for a combination of relaxation and "thinking like a fish." I would go so far as to say that they are actually describing a bit of shamanic experience: the thrill of losing their everyday ego awareness for a few hours while living in the world of Fish. They seem to be transported and entering into the rush of water over stone with the complete freedom to focus only on where the fish are hiding and what they are biting as the fishermen stand in the cold stream and baking sun.

Robyn Bridges

Whether or not you are a dedicated fisherman, any kind of personal experience with a river can be powerful. The memories of it can linger for years, a fluid remembrance moving through your life. Rivers remind us to pay attention to how we belong and to remember the flow of life in our physical bodies. I wrote the following poem the day of renewal at the banks of the Gallatin River.

River Songs

Today I travel to the river alone,
 trying to remember how I belong.
Each drop of water plays out and down
 and past me, notes I need to hear
 and may never hear again.
The music strengthens my spirit;
 celestial sounds caress from the wet belly of the earth.
Sounds melt around each waiting rock into my body,
Become my own sounds,
Until I begin to sing back to the river its own song
 and the river sings me.
No one can take this away—
 not my mother or sister or
 anyone who has found me wrong.
The secret cave of my abandoned self joins the great flow,
And the river invites a joining, a dancing, a falling silent,
With the ears only the river and I know,
A water chord rising to the sound of my long attention.

11

Fire in the Earth

Our lives now center on experience and the fire of its consuming.
—David Whyte, "Millennium"

The Yellowstone National Park fires of 1988 were the most devastating the park had ever known. Miles and miles of scorched and parched land resulted. Local and even national newspapers were full of the chronicles. However, few accounts detailed or even mentioned the horror and suffering of the many animal residents of the park who could not flee the whiplash of the shifting flames. Park rangers confided in acquaintances of mine that the smell of rotting animal flesh was so unbearable they had to wear facemasks while scouring certain areas. Most animals who had been caught in the fires, from squirrels to buffalo, were found dead, but some were still barely alive and in agony. Most of those mercifully received a bullet to the head, a resounding answer to the fire's fierce swath.

Throughout that parched summer, the policy debate over whether or not to let the fires burn raged as hot as the fires themselves, yet it did little to affect the acres of charred land that resulted. Blackened stumps of once-luxurious trees and prairie undergrowth changed the face of the landscape for most of the lifetimes of current visitors as well as altering the habitat for the remaining animal residents. Many tall charred trees, black and bare, still stand as sober testaments to the power of the element of fire.

Reseeding and planting aside, growth is still slow. Years later, signs still dot the blackened landscape reading "Growth since the 1988 Fires," showing small seedlings and saplings trying hard to fill the shoes of their predecessors. With our short growing season in the high mountain country, the land will take a long time to replenish itself. Even twenty years later, miles of still-charred forests blanket the land like a dead hand fallen with fingers up.

My own tendency focused on the morose and sorrowful roots in the memory of those fires. The smoke reached us ninety miles north in the Gallatin Valley (once known as the "Valley of Flowers"), and I choked on the un-oxygenated air. While others extolled the excitement and rational reasons why such a fire was necessary and long overdue, I curled up in a ball of sorrow, feeling in my own body the fate of the animals who could not escape. The victim archetype looms large for all animal lovers in these harsh conditions. For any of us who have suffered, even in the slightest, from our own physical or emotional blows, the devastation burns close to home. I allowed the bleak scenery to find a match in my own fire-blighted memory of a past burnt beyond recognition, a once-fertile life seared by life's hot blasts. I too have had short growing seasons. Acres of my own life still stand somber and quiet, blackened and slow to recover. As poet David Whyte soberly reminds us, when fire rages, our lives center around the all-consuming harshness of experience.

As I have learned, however, life becomes bearable, and ultimately powerful, when we let fire burn us through to redemption. The act of forgiveness provides a salve from the fierce heat of living, and allows us to include a perception of being refined as well as being charred. Refining means that we allow our own life sorrows to burn a path to our hearts, to ignite our sense of compassion, and to spur us to action. As a result of such scorching heat, growth is revealed in the better way we treat others and ourselves. We can live the rest of our lives like a burnt stump or become part of the new life stretching up through the undergrowth.

In the process, we do not become only light and happy, denying the dark. The dark burn is what gives nutrients to the soil to enrich our new lives and lends character and a richly authentic texture to our personalities. We do not normally choose to start fires of undesired change, but we can learn to persevere through them. We can access a deep soulfulness as we let these experiences teach us and make us wiser, more real, deeper, and more compassionate. The gift of the burning experience arrives when we fully acknowledge the contribution of fire as a type of metaphor: salvation through clearing the way for new growth.

Losses such as the passing of unmet desires in our lives can challenge our sense of redemption. As we age, we begin to realize that certain dreams that were time-sensitive may never come to pass. My own simple but consuming dream of having an intact family was an example, but everyone has his or her own version. Something has gone awry in our lives; how to pick up the pieces and go on is the challenge. When any of us meet our Waterloo, a great grieving process may then be in store for us. If we take it head-on, we can come through the other side as stronger, more accepting, and more multidimensional human beings. However, if we avoid the grieving directly and instead fall into denial, blaming, addictions, or other avoidances to quell our fear of the process, we only add another burden to the one from which we're trying to get free. Maybe we do a bit of both over time: some real grieving and some avoidance.

I keep attempting to attend to grieving fully so that I can truly move on. I have learned how to let nature assist me in doing so.

My dream of being a mother to healthy, normally attached children and enjoying a strong marriage eroded. Upon divorcing, local pastors assured me I was going to hell and while I was still alive could never remarry. Some who I thought were friends judged me for leaving the marriage and faded away. Even my family pulled away, the one place I thought would always be a source of sustenance. Only now, even more years later, do I realize that the long periods of depression I experienced were perhaps a way to avoid the actual grieving process. Caving into myself was a way of denying reality and a refusal to accept the circumstances. Through feeling burned by the thoughtless preachers who told me I was hell-bound, my own stubbornness created a burn area fueled by anger and disappointment. Though in an odd way feeling depressed protected me, I imagine I would have healed faster if I had been less resistant to inevitable change. My grief became a smoldering fire that was never quite extinguished, keeping the soil from cooling and new life from growing. Metaphorically, I actually needed the element of a strong, complete fire to destroy my old landscape and form new soil for my desire to live. Eventually, three years of personal counseling with a gifted therapist and one new soul friend provided the way. My own inner landscape began to find new growth and to thrive once again.

Fire is forceful, definite, and strong. These are good qualities when activated at the right times and in the right amounts. Chinese culture teaches that of all the elements on earth, fire can be the most powerful. They speak of us as individually needing either more or less of this element in our thoughts and personalities. Some of us need more fire in our lives to spark us because we are lethargic or depressed; others need less because their own heat burns both themselves and others. The appropriate amount of inner fire can change over a person's life and with circumstance. The trick is to know when to let it burn and when to contain it. If we are to live responsibly, we must hold personal and communal council to determine the right amounts of this robust element.

Time can heal, at least to a certain extent, and so can the caring acts of friends and family. These days I find myself looking as much at the new young greenery in life as at the old charred stumps. I finally see that all things renew themselves, that the dance of life goes on because it desires to, and that the other elements around it create the environment for it to do so. As I come into relationships in my own life of nurture, shelter, fecundity, and the moisture of caring, nature provides the nutrients for a return from the devastation of loss to the recovery of spirit. These days I keen after beauty and loveliness. These days I am no longer interested in the religion of a preacher's threats of a fiery hell. I am only interested in redemption as the result of life's fierce embrace and new growth peeking out from charred land.

12

The Power of Place

As humans we require places as support for our spirit ... We never speak of an environment we have known; it is always places we have known and recall. We are homesick for places, we are reminded of places, it is the sounds and smells and sights of places which haunt us and against which we measure our present.

—Alan Gussow

Belonging to a place is an essential need for every living thing. Animals live in certain environments that support their diets, offer shelter, and provide safety from predators. Plants belong to the environment that proffers them just the right amount of sun, rain, and soil. As humans, in addition to having our physical needs met, we also have an often unrecognized need to belong to our world of physicality through emotional, mental, or spiritual connections. In Gussow's quote above, he speaks of places haunting us; they echo a deep longing when we have ignored them too long. It is as if their spirits return to call us back to a connection we abandoned, a place to connect with again for nurturing and sustenance.

Human nature includes a reflective capacity, which provides potential for soulful fulfillment. As many of the world's cultures have acknowledged for centuries, we are drawn to revisit physical places that reactivate higher functions of ourselves—places such as the pyramids in Egypt, the great cathedrals of Western Europe, old Celtic stone circles, the Taj Mahal. Many revere these as sacred places, ones that carry a felt sense of reverence, worship, magic, and mystery. I consider that what makes a place sacred is a combination of the natural energy of that place and the types of worshipful human recognition it has received over time. One of Western psychology's founders, Abraham Maslow, posited that our struggle to live well metaphorically takes the shape of a pyramid. At the long base of the triangle are our basic needs for food, water, safety, and shelter. Only when these needs are met can we move up the pyramid to develop a healthy ego and become of real service in the world. If or when we arrive at the pinnacle, we have sufficiently gained a base that supports us in realizing our higher functions of self-actualization and a vital spirituality. In modern life, when we awaken to our inner life, we may be shocked to realize that while busy meeting our base need to survive, we had neglected to thrive. A remedy is to connect with a specific physical place in nature that renews and restores soul. This helps set our sights toward the bigger picture of life and our part within it.

Any time we become stressed, we need solace for the soul. Solace can be found in any place that nourishes and connects us to the beauty of the earth. We may find a relaxing sacred spot or one that releases a wild beauty within ourselves. These places can be as quiet and simple as a tree in Central Park in New York City or as dramatic as a deep gorge cascading off the Beartooth Mountains in Montana. It could even be a canal along the edge of a country road that shuttles water into a nearby field. All may include tranquil or evocative elements of nature as well as plants, animals, open stretches of earth, and a respite from machine noise. In these places, our minds let go of the obsessive need to try to control our lives or to figure everything out. As we allow nature to quell our restlessness, the essence of a place informs us of deeper, quieter things.

The power of place is evident in its ability to move us into a meditative state, where we allow nature to become our teacher. Our pulse slows and regulates, and our breathing deepens. Our senses awake to the fecundity of everything around us. We become students in an outdoor classroom.

As we listen deeply, we find that our bodies take in a different type of knowledge than that to which our minds are normally accustomed, and our souls begin to attend to patterns that are more creative and less traveled.

I have found a few key places where my soul life is recharged and my courage for living restored. Most of them are in the mountains, which hold great stories and deep wisdom. They always assist me in remembering the larger story of all of life, as opposed to the sometimes too large story of my own small life. Mountains make me feel cared for and watched over, like benevolent parents lovingly watching their grown child. One of my favorite spots is quite accessible, just up the road from where I live. This piece of land is the same 160-acre slope bordering Forest Service land and the Bridger Mountains where I first really listened to the "Stone People." The Bridgers are a very gently sloping, approachable, and friendly range, with an entire Ridge Trail for hikers and runners that traverses the length of the north-south contour. "The Property," as I have come to proudly call it (though I don't own it; my rancher friend Harry does), rests on the far northwest slope of the Bridgers. It includes an easement trail for hikers and horseback riders to cover the mere mile of land to reach the Forest Service boundary. Harry's cows graze on the 160 acres of herbicide-free land I have grown to love. Of course, I patronize Harry's Half-Circle Pride ranch business. In fact, when friends come to dinner and I am serving beef, they generally ask, "Are we having Harry's cows for dinner tonight?"

The first time I wandered up into this lovely property, snow was receding, with dirt-laden clumps hiding only behind the largest boulders and pines. I shivered with winter's last reminders but forgot the chill on my skin as I became immersed in the energy of the place itself. I had to cinch up my hiking boots to more securely traverse the ups and downs of the multitude of small and large moss and green lichen rocks. So many in number, they left just enough soil between them to be lightly dotted with early spring wildflowers: shiny pink, soft white, and striated violet. I alternated between bending down to touch the rock's cold surfaces and caress the wildflowers, and then straightening up to soak in the valley below. The long-distance view astounded me: to the south and west lay the entire greening Gallatin Valley, dotted with too many buildings. Yet from a distance, they looked less offensive, offset by sparkling blue ribbons of water winding through. And the entire valley, hugged by all my favorite mountain ranges, including the Bridgers right behind me, formed an energetic embrace that curled my shoulders closer to each other. While appreciating my surroundings, I began to reflect on my life: what was working, what was not, the ways I needed to feel better. Yet the farther up the slope I traveled, the more I could feel my own thoughts, worries, and cares sliding off my back as a child might playfully slip down the soft moss-rocks dotting the hillside.

I began to "hear" the surrounding tumble of rocks and boulders deep in the middle of some age-old conversation. Their language was not one my mind could specifically translate, but my body and soul understood with a thrill of recognition, of memory, and of a deep, solid knowing. I became still within myself and alive with the richness of everything around me. It was on this very day that I looked skyward and first officially met a spiritual group I now call the "Grandmothers and Grandfathers," who I realized I had met years before, but at that time I did not understand quite who they were. Then, I had simply looked up in the middle of appreciating all around me, imagined I saw their long, tall forms circled in a group, and just knew they were "mine." This time I heard them clearly, identified them individually, and listened to each of their stories about themselves, my history with them, and the ways we had agreed before I even came to earth that they would support and encourage me during this difficult experience of life.

They continue to refresh and inspire me in all aspects of my life.

During the first few years of having discovered The Property, I imagined that someday the owner might sell and that perhaps I could afford to buy it. I knew I would treat it with the kindness, reverence, and lack of development it deserved. Like a child in a toy shop, I had soon picked out a spot for my dream home, envisioning where, after the hammering carpenters and cement-pouring trucks had completed their feats, I would live the rest of my days in serene content, even if it was a compensation for a life of disappointed dreams. While picking my way across the small and large boulders laying across the land, however, I fell prey to the development disease, also adding a retreat center with four or five cabins, a lodge for dining, and a separate log building for the retreat meetings themselves. I would facilitate several of the gatherings myself, and I saw other healers from around the world arriving in the beautiful "valley of flowers" (before it became the "valley of the big box stores") to offer their wisdom, along with mine, to eager groups. Yet as the years have passed and the price of land has soared, my hopes of ever owning a piece of this magical place have dwindled. I have grieved this loss of a now-improbable future and have learned to content myself with just being able to hike on the land whenever I want to. Most days, that is enough.

Every time I set foot on The Property, I begin with a feast of the senses through the touch of the moss-rocks and the feel in my body as I climb up and over the many small rocks on the trail. My eyes scope the junipers and the widening valley views as I gain elevation. I inhale the pungent smell of the air, wet with the large streams cascading out of the north end of the draw. Soon I diverge from the trail to hike through uneven ground of tufted grasses and sparse wildflowers, between secure and loose rocks, up short rises and down long drainages spilling out of the mountain. From the higher elevation, I can turn around and take in the whole Gallatin Valley. I watch clouds roll in over the Tobacco Root Mountains to the west, turn to see the Bridger range behind me, and turn again toward the Gallatin range to the south, smiling in remembrance of all my adventures in each range. My home valley, dotted with houses and communities not yet quite running into each other, seems less developed than I usually see it from a lower-elevation perspective. From higher ground, the view of still-undeveloped land is vast and quiet. The new big box stores are merely small blights in comparison to the open spaces nearby; here I cannot smell the exhaust of the cars from the roadways. Buildings look insignificant and unreal, dots on a picture postcard. I feel decidedly smug from my preferred viewpoint, standing amidst the dusty smells of juniper, chirping birds, and the good earth.

Every time I go to that special place, I learn something about myself. Usually, I take away a teaching that helps me rebalance my life or encourages me in some aspect of living. One time it was an answer to a specific problem I had; another time, it was a robin (the connection did not escape me) that kept alighting on a boulder right in front of me. Each time I have found it easy to make meaning out of what is being "said" because I've become very quiet within myself, willing to listen and to believe the answer. Doubters may call it "imagination" and skeptics "self-deception," but my experiences have taught me to be reverential of the power of a special place as a living other and the great gifts it offers. It is real because it effects real change: it always enhances my life and improves my attitude. I am a better person because of it.

Physical theories have been developed that may satisfy those who doubt the interconnectedness of animate and inanimate matter, as Fritjof Capra has made clear in his books *The Tao of Physics* and *The Turning Point*. Nature, he explains in great detail, like the atoms that make up all matter, is engaged in a constant flow of related activity, and we would find ways of living in better harmony by heeding the patterns already in evidence. Quantum physics is constantly revealing more evidence that Everything is truly alive and connected.

The connection of humans to physical place in nature is deep. Some places tend to be perceived as sacred because of their history of human worship as well as the energy they carry. These places can move and transform people, opening them to a sense of the divine within and without. Other places simply sustain their own purity. A friend of mine once told me that the natural places that have the clearest voice for us are the locations that have not been lied to by humans. *Not lied to.* I have never forgotten that. After pondering his statement, I have come to understand it to mean that the land is intrinsically honest, and where that energy has remained undisturbed by betrayal (mining, pollution, development, and the resulting human foibles), it can still transmit the power of its original clarity.

You can still find your god, goddess, creator, or whatever you call that which is greater than yourself in any place. However, I tend to believe that sacred places carry a special charge that many humans recognize. We may enhance this power through our own intent and worshipful infusions. Yet the fact that one's own private places in nature have perhaps never been worshipped by another person is also quite thrilling, because you can feel free to create your own template with the energy there without any other human input. It is lovely to go to a prescribed place of community worship, like a church, temple, or Native ceremonial gathering, but having your own private, sacred place provides you with a sense of personal responsibility to your creator. Another benefit is that if you were one of several siblings, you can finally get your only-child fantasy fulfilled! Just you and God. The universe is not without a sense of humor.

What keeps us from going to sacred places of respite and renewal more often than we do? Our understandably busy lives, of course. But at a more spiritual level, as we lose touch over time with our own wild, intimate, and unpredictable natures, the power of such places may be too intimidating to approach. I have felt this in myself at times, unable to sally my soul up to such greatness. Being in a powerful place is like breathing into the heart of God; it requires a kind of willingness to be vulnerable enough to see and be seen on a much deeper level than those of your mundane cares. The spiritual encounter of place will take you on its own uncharted journey, and you never know ahead of time quite where you will go on the inner planes or when you will be back. As exciting as it is to be in the wilderness, our psyches intrinsically know that they will have to surrender control and have to trust something greater than themselves. It takes a secure psyche to let go, to employ a sense of right timing, and as mythology teacher Joseph Campbell would say, to find "a willingness to answer the call of the hero's journey." Each visit to a sacred place is a type of embarkation into an underworld and inner world. If the journey has been successful, as Campbell explains, we will emerge with gifts of understanding and a better way of living our lives.

Being connected to a place implies you are in relationship with it. The more you are personally inspired and renewed by a place, the stronger your connection. Like any relationship, the more it gives to you what you need, the fonder you become of it. This even includes a sense of balance (do you spend too much or too little time there?) and interaction (do you only take, or do you give back what you can—gratitude, donations, or perhaps work for the protection of open spaces?). While our shadow sides can overindulge in the narcissism of constantly using place as a bandage for our wounds, our healing selves know how to access these sacred places to make us better people in the world: more capable, resourceful, contemplative, thoughtful, and better able to attend to the needs of others. As we connect with the whole of life, we learn to live in a more inclusive manner and care for everything around us, from plants to animals to people. Sacred places teach us to care.

Understanding the power of place means that we can be enriched, enlivened, and perhaps a little more enlightened; we can begin to live in a fuller, more interactive, and more caring manner. The power of place becomes evident as we become vulnerable to its strength. It takes a strong person to be aware of the power in the place that surrounds him or her because it can be so vast and threatening to the ego that thinks itself the center. In finding place, we become naturally more balanced, finding encouragement and solace.

Helpful messages are always available to the listening ear and wisdom to the stilled mind in a place that carries power, whether a private or publically recognized site. May you find or revisit your own place of power soon and open to all it has to offer.

13
The Fairy Councils

The wee folk are the ones we long for; their gossamer wings carry us forward when we have lost our way ...
—Fairy Clan tribute

I am not in Ireland right now, the fabled land of the fairies, but I have visited that damp and rainy island and think I have almost seen a few of them. Now I am in dry southwest Montana in the changing month of May. Even though May is considered late spring, because of our northern latitude, the brown winter grasses are just starting to get pushed out by new green volunteers. I am sitting on the back porch of a lovely and luxurious handcrafted cabin at stunning Alta Meadow Ranch. Today the ranch, as I have come to blithely call it (as though it were my own), carries the simple beauty of an open mountain meadow with a slow-moving river, a pristine quiet, and a strong morning sun. I am keen to see my beloved moose, who could appear at the edge of the meadow at any moment, and my heart beats faster in anticipation. The red-winged blackbirds gurgle their mating songs while taking turns hogging the bird feeder near the porch.

Suddenly I hear a great rhythmic rush of squeaked flapping and cavorting over to my left, as a lone Canada goose streams low by me, deftly disappearing in the large willows dotting the middle of the meadow. If it were a cold or foggy morning, I might be in a morose mood and imagine the goose had lost a mate and that it would fly around all day, incessantly looking for her. But today, with the sun warming my upturned face, I imagine only that he is returning from a nest site exploration to the flock at the south end of the meadow, who have temporarily beached by the marsh pond. Though he disappears from sight quickly, I soon hear the greeting (or territorial annoyance) calls of his flock as he alights.

He has landed. And so have I, weary traveler of life's too many mundane requirements. Too much tending my small acreage miles away from here and paying bills and working and trying to remember to breathe during this inexplicably difficult Mother's Day weekend.

Some holidays sneak up on you just when you had forgotten to care. Others may pass without as much as a twinge. Some holidays are eagerly anticipated, with the anticipation well met, and the resulting memories warm and sweet. Other times, probably at the discretion of our vast unconscious, a holiday looms like an unwelcome storm, tremors rumoring the quakes to come.

My own childlessness, being infertile even through all my inner fecundity rising with each passing year, formed an odd pairing. I never birthed a child, so could never say "Oh, that was the most amazing experience of my life," though I have birthed a tremendous appreciation for the magic of the natural world. I will never say, "My children are the most precious gift" or "Yes, I have grandchildren," though I have many godchildren who have chosen me over the years, asking, "If anything ever happens to my mom, would you be mine?"

The children my husband and I had adopted as toddlers never completely bonded with us, their early abuse being too severe. We gave everything we had, and it was still not enough. As their pathology grew, so did our terror and stark disappointment as the bizarre and sometimes dangerous behaviors of two of the three required them to be returned to state care. However, our youngest, by the time he was twenty, eventually found some measure of closeness with me. My heart was glad in a vaguely distant manner, like seeing a welcome moose on the horizon that sleeks away into wooded cover too soon, and I would be left with an open palate once again.

With such soul shock, a shiver of dashed dreams, and such unexpected human disappointment, colors fade and all becomes a washed-out pastel.

Yet after seasons of darkness, even feeling a storm is better than feeling nothing at all.

How does this willingness to feel life again come about? I learned to listen to my instinctual body. I welcomed what wanted to be invited in again and kicked out what needed to be kicked out. I finally began to breathe in living, just as it was, a little by choice and a little by grace. I learned to love life again.

I have learned enough about the times of shivering to be nonjudgmental for feeling the shudder. The early times when I could not feel anything were the bleakest; holidays were lost in an indistinct blur of gray nothing. Now at least when I feel the shudder coming, I let myself thrill to the soul having its way with me, living a life that I now allow to be inhabited. Through doing so, I find that more healing has taken place than I had imagined. I am more present to my truth and abandon myself less often.

I hear the ranch managers' diesel pick-up approaching my cabin long before I see it, a welcome sound because it carries the people I have grown to love. They and their two lovely girls are hospitable, warm, and inviting, and the stories they've told me about all their years of experience in the backcountry fill my already fertile imagination with more fodder to feed next winter's boredom. They have also become friends, all of us sharing joys and heartaches, our love of the land, and a commonality of spirit refreshed by the natural world.

"Deb!" I fling open the door and wrap my arms around her like she is a long-lost traveler just returning home from the Himalayas. More accurately, I am.

"Robyn, welcome back." Her dark hair and twinkling eyes welcome me right into this place of meadow and mountains and magic. We talk about the moose mommies and babies they've seen again this spring, the wolf situation, the geese. I ask if she and her Irish husband Beattie have been to the Fairy Council Rocks, a picturesque and massive clump of moss rocks at the end of the traveled road.

"Yes, we have. And guess what?" she giggles. "Beattie was riding his mountain bike past them the other day and just as he was passing, the crossbars broke and he took a real header. Really banged up his head." She grins mischievously. "Do you suppose the fairies were trying to tell him something?"

"Of course," I respond, like a paid tour guide to the area. "He was probably ignoring them, and you have to pay penance or they'll trip you up."

"What do you suppose he'll have to do next time?" She baits me, awaiting my reply.

"Acknowledge them, of course," I tell her in my most matter-of-fact tone. "He'll just have to nod without interrupting their council, and then they should let him pass, no problem."

"Good," she says solemnly, the hint of a smile on her lips. "I'll be sure to tell him."

The Fairy Council Rocks, as I have named them (though I prefer to think that the fair folk themselves planted the name they wanted in my mind), encompasses a large, steep expanse of sheer mountain height punctuated by trickles of water that form beds of the loveliest shades of lime to deep, forest-green moss harboring little tiny clover leaves with tinier white petal flowers, and it sports ledges, everywhere ledges. After meditatively gazing at them, I decided the ledges must be the lodging places for the fairy beds, and the actual council was likely the larger, more open concave rock opening. I'm quite sure fairies and their councils exist all over the world, and I suspect that this particular place draws those from the quieter side of habitation, the ones who prefer to dwell far from human existence.

It is not as social a feel as other council sites I have come across around the world. Certain locations, tucked away in groves of trees and cave-like settings, have a sense of laughter, stories, and a great twittering and flapping of wings. Others are more somber and wise. This one seems to me to be of a more private nature, and I consider that fairies might also have realms of varied reasons for councils. All have a sense of government to them, a sense of order and decisions being made. That's how the fairy realm has been able to remain intact as long as it has. Trust me about this information; I don't know how, but I seem to know.

The older I get, the more confident of certain things I am. Some I grow less sure of, like why all beings suffer so deeply, but I am more sure than ever about the wee folk. Perhaps the "other side" spirits gain importance as I feel my clay body drying out, just as my once-young body, with spirit fresh from the heavens, was still getting used to itself. However, as my body moves to the other side of midlife and as my skin begins to dry, my soul becomes more moist, as does my connection with the other world. I have finally let myself realize what some of our young people today have already grown up knowing: an entire invisible realm actually inhabits our very same earth. All kinds of beings, from devas to angels, surround us so much more often than we know! Such habitation is good and makes the rigors of living so much more acceptable. My imaginal escape, the skeptic might say. My real and distinct privilege, I say. It seems to me that fairies are more beneficial to humans than the mischievous or downright mean ones portrayed by fearful old Irish stories, but perhaps I am connected to the helpful beings simply because they are the ones who have chosen *me*. At any rate, fairies and other invisibles exist, no matter how they are acknowledged, and they have stronger and more sentient power than they are generally given credit for. If we approach them with desire, faith, and respect, they respond with magic and mystery and levels of help and encouragement for our denser bodies and slower spirit awareness. Some of these delightful, light creatures are even being recorded these days on digital cameras, hoaxes aside, in images that neither photographers or scientists have yet been able to disprove.

The welfare of the Fairy Council Rocks at the end of the traveled road continues to receive attention from Deb and me as we talk on about it and our sense of soul and spirit in our lives. Finally we move on to family details and what caused me to suddenly call them up and appear at the cabin two days later. I am brief in my response about my Mother's Day distress, solid with the truth but not liquefying into victimhood. That much I have learned: to avoid the bogs when I can. No sense slushing my hooves into that heavy muck and then having trouble heaving myself out. There have been enough occasions when I have gotten lost in sorrow unwittingly or even by intent, which now I realize all served their purpose at the time. However, I am no longer some one-year-old juvenile moose awkwardly careening through the treacherous bogs. I am a mature adult and know how to pick my way through. I have grown.

Deb departs to return to her ranch house and the endless chores, promising to return later for an afternoon walk to the Fairy Grove. I quickly unpack and then slowly settle into the swing on the back porch, sipping tea and marveling at my great good fortune to have arranged nothing more pressing to do this week than some light reading, to periodically scan the horizon for the moose who sometimes cross the meadow, and to listen to the birds newly arrived from spring migration. I have brought a mystery novel with me and have become too engrossed in the characters and possible clues of suspicious people to take the time to go back into the cabin for a refill of tea. Suddenly something catches the edge of my vision, like soft, twinkling fairy lights around a larger substance. At the same time I hear a soft laugh overlaying a subtle rhythmic reverberation, a kind of *thub-thubbing* noise, not so much the sound of light hooves but rather the way a gelding's stomach rumbles as he trots. Visually, I pick up a kind of streaking, the way you can swear you saw something dark pass across your vision, but when you blink, it is gone.

I blink, and lucky for me, the vision is still there, several yards in front of me and off to my left—a yearling moose moving fast yet uncertainly, running as though Mom had kicked him out of the area so she could take care of her new baby. A moose! The mangy youngster was well fed but wet from a probable early morning swim, with tatters of matted winter hair begging to fall off. Though his fast trot carried him effortlessly forward, his instinctual body and backward glances seemed to be urging him to turn around, back to Mother, even though he knew he would be rebuffed again. The confusion in his eyes was apparent, with traces of hurt, but an urgency to keep moving was even stronger. The older sibling must always experience this when younger ones come along. Never having had a sibling younger than myself, I didn't quite know his experience, but I was still sorry he had to go through it, and from the wrenching feeling in my own heart, I was sure that I understood his angst.

His familial drama aside, the moment of the young moose's appearance was thrilling and ended too soon. Within thirty seconds, he had completed his dash from the willows at the middle of the meadow to the far north side, disappearing once again in the willows upstream, heading up the Deer Creek drainage, which I knew all the moose in the area loved. I darted off the porch, trying to follow him to the edge of the meadow with my version of an oblique, unobtrusive running walk, but he lost me even faster. This alone reminded me that he was capable, he would survive this loss, he could move into the next phase of his life because he was naturally equipped to do so. Was I? I hoped that by moving close to his energy field, I might find my own instinctual ability to thrive through coming apart, through dissolution and disillusion. If that young moose could do it, I—constantly communing with "other" in nature, in reading about and learning the wisdom of so many ancestors before me—I could too. The young moose careened over a long bench of grasses and was gone. I marveled. If I had popped inside the cabin just for a moment to get more tea, I would have missed the whole show.

After he left, I returned to the porch, leaning over the log railing, and watched the air in the meadow for a long time, feeling how it had recorded every passing wisp of his leggy movement, silently hiding it. I even sniffed the air for any possible hint of his scent, laughing at my arrogance that I could be that good of a coyote. I spent the rest of the morning with my book closed, quietly surveying the habitable meadow from my comfortable swing chair, contemplating the day as it passed and the sun as it traveled effortlessly over a patient blue, cloud-dotted sky. The Fairy Council and Lodges would have to wait for me to visit them until later in the day. For now, the meadow had all my attention, and I willingly anchored my fairy soul to it.

Part II

The Medicine of Animals, Plants, and Place

There are two ways to live your life. One is as though nothing is a miracle. The other is as though everything is a miracle.
—Albert Einstein

Part II of *Moose Medicine* chronicles a series of personal realizations as a direct result of moose and other animal encounters that led me to open my heart and mind to the sometimes more subtle teachings of plants and place. Some of my epiphanies have come directly from observing the unaffected ways animals live; others have been inspired by what I call "free attention" during my hours of outdoor adventures, including time in my own backyard.

Though I have had many amazing spiritual experiences with moose and other living beings, I don't expect that adventure should always happen when I am in nature; I am happiest when I simply allow synchronicity of sightings and experience rather than look for or expect a close encounter with any numinous aspect of the natural world. As a wise therapist once reminded me, "Do not seek experience. Merely be present. Show up, and if you perceive God coming to you, fine. If not, then you have just shown up for God." So I show up, and what happens, happens—or not. When our spirits are open, we are able to realize the teachings and blessings of any outcome, no matter the level of drama.

While you read the following section, your own insights and experiences will certainly have their own unique response in tandem with your soul's evolution. These accounts are how my journey has been unfolding. I hope you find the stories helpful, ones that activate and support your own.

14

Returning to the Open Trails

Nature will reveal itself if we will only look.
—Thomas Edison

I arrive for an appointment at a client's home up scenic Jackson Creek, in the heart of the Bridger Mountains in southwest Montana. Years ago I rode a gentleman's unruly Tennessee Walkers—or rather, they rode me—all over these rolling high country hills. As I climbed aboard, they would enthusiastically grab the bits in their mouths and fly at out-of-control speeds around bogs and old barns and up to the tops of steep hills until finally their slowing gait would allow me to catch my breath. At the summit, the bit would finally seem to work, and we would stop to gaze around. Mountains rolled outward below us, undulating in front of and behind each other in shades of blue and gray. Homes peeking through groves of trees dotted the valley below. With the slightest breeze, the blues of the sky would shift their hue, from light blue to deep azure.

While recovering from the Walkers' fast pace, I always felt amazement that horses were such instinctive animals of flight, their fast footfalls still reverberating in my young adult body. As I gazed around me, I would feel a developing sense of the beauty of place and a somehow familiar kinship to the vast panorama of open space. The horse and I would soon carry on through meadows and streams. We would shiver together when coming around a bend to find moose foraging in a boggy, willowed meadow, and

I would yearn for more time to stare at them while my horse would reel away. For hours I would marvel at nature from the fast pace set by my energetic four-legged friend.

As my career developed, I found myself spending less time in horseplay or viewing moose and more time working, traveling to various clients' mountain homes. Maturing life began to require more time earning income, and the practicality of doing so overrode the urgency I used to feel to adventure outdoors. Gone were the more carefree days of youth. Yet now, even in the act of driving through vast acreages of forest and meadow, I begin to recall the intimacy of the natural world I have been neglecting.

Today, after giving a session to a homebound client who lives deep in the Bangtail Mountains of southwest Montana, I am ready to once again breathe in the surrounding quiet, to see and be seen. I am alert to the herd of elk disappearing over the north ridge and even to the modest welcoming grasses from the barrow pit that draw my gaze to the grass field beyond.

Rather than going home directly, I drive a short distance to a game trail I spotted on the way up the canyon. I pull off the road to reconnect with the nature I've been neglecting. Shyly, almost virginally, I move through my temporary fear of the intimacy I know awaits. My eager fingers betray that reserve as I fumble to secure my hiking boots. Soon I am padding up a seldom-walked trail. Then I, like the elk over the ridge, disappear from view into the heart of the welcoming wilds, my limbs beginning to swing free as if another older, yet younger, life once again possesses them.

I am present now, alive to each moment. I pay attention. Everything around me seems to be in conversation; the trees are bent in acknowledgment. Even the soil on the trail converses with itself, testament to a solid and fecund life. The path is strong enough to support me but interactive enough to be changed by my footprints. Distinct hoof marks tell me that deer, elk, and moose have walked this trail often, and it offers great pleasure to know that those same creatures will pass this way again long after I have left. The stones and moss-rocks seemingly tossed in disarray onto the grasses on either side of the trail are deep in hushed communion; if I listen, I might hear their foreign yet somehow familiar language. I feel the remembered hum of a rhythm different from my own yet of which I am a part. I feel myself leaving ordinary time, my mind relaxing as it becomes a blank slate. Gratefully, thankfully, I carefully pick my way into the earth's pulse and the slow beat of her very patient heart. It soothes my own, and I breathe the relief of coming home. My story to the earth of all the reasons I haven't been there for so long begins to pour out.

Soon, the story of my life doesn't matter anymore. It has been received, and that is that. I am now clear, in a state of free attention. Now I can be present to all around me, to revel through the red willow bushes in moose habitat, to allow sorrow to fade away and joy to overtake me. I do so with a slight tilt of my head and a slowing of my pace. The buzz and hum all around sends me into its own life, its own rhythm, and I am at one with the flies and the lupine and the wild iris.

And then, of course because I don't expect it, I round the trail to come face-to-face with a large, sandy-brown moose. I stop, inert, caught in midstride. Facing me directly, she doesn't move; for a moment, not a muscle of hers or mine twitches. I think she is a lone female without a calf to protect; a female because of her gentle tolerance, and without a calf, also because of her gentle tolerance! We are so close I could almost touch her. Her whiskers around her muzzle twitch softly; she gazes through her unusually large eyes at me and beyond, as though looking for ... what? Surely she heard my careless footsteps ahead of time and, having four times the olfactory capacity of a dog, smelled me coming. And yet she remained right on the trail, neither aggressive nor afraid. I am transfixed with excitement and fear; I think I hear the pounding of another set of hooves approaching. I imagine an irate bull moose coming to rescue his mate and frantically turn my head to look behind me. Nothing. Just empty trail. With a wry smile, I realize once again, as I often do in exciting moments when I'm the only human around, that the pounding is only my loudly beating heart. I muffle a laugh through pursed lips. I am still inert, standing midstride. After a moment, the big, attractive cow moose flares her nostrils at me, steps off the trail, and disappears into the willows. I am left nervously laughing, looking around like a child caught doing something I shouldn't have. But I would do it again, in a second.

How much I need this! When I neglect going to the mountains, it is the same as growing distant in any intimate human relationship. Over time, distance tends to support a denial of the intimacy once shared. But I am not distant from nature anymore. The natural world is always ready to welcome a return. Any of us can always walk right back onto forested trails and find connection again.

I walk on for another hour or so with no more encounters of the large kind: only bouncing nuthatches and singing vireos. I am lost in thought now, realizing the consciousness of nature as a living and sentient entity directly. This of course opposes the dominant worldview that we are separate from nature and meant to rule over it. I have become a student of the practice of deep ecology: the call to identification with and action for preservation of nature, with humans as only one part of the whole. Building upon indigenous knowing, deep ecology takes the wider, connected view both of earth-based religions and of the progressive science of quantum physics. Both spiritually and scientifically, humans are seen as intricately interconnected with nature, not separate from or superior to it. As naturalist Aldo Leopold noted, we are "plain citizens," not masters of other species.

The ability to benefit in our own bodies from nature through a kind of physical spirituality engages effortlessly if we do not resist what we hear and see. We simply let the impressions of the world enliven us. Even touching stones, we can forget our physical selves, becoming one with the hard surfaces of mossy rocks. We can feel their ancient pulse and see the world through their presence. We can become absorbed in the "not I" of their essence.

Some cultures call this moving into the essence of another life or reality "shamanic," a temporary moving into the totality of another's being. This shape-shifting ability may be accessible to anyone who keenly desires intimate knowledge of another's life force. The trick is to thoroughly become the other life form yet still be able to comfortably and completely return to self. Great relief awaits if you are able to allow the otherness of nature to absorb you. You slip into another's skin, whether that of a tree, a stone, or a wild animal, let it teach and revitalize you, and then by an act of will return to your everyday human self. I can teach you how.

If you visit a wild and private place to which you are drawn (whether in the future by an actual foray into the wilds, your memory, or your imagination even now as you read), breathe deeply and take time to acquaint yourself with that place. Notice all the sensory detail around you: the curve of that leaf, the feel of that tree root, the sound of the wind in the trees or the stream rushing by. As you realize you are moving into an altered experience that on some level is beyond your control, some trepidation is natural. It is like the excitement we felt as children when about to embark on a neighborhood adventure. If you never felt this as a child, it is not too late. It is never too late. You feel the excitement as fear and a welcome draw and move right on in. Continue to breathe deeply and well ... Take your time ... Let your thoughts of home, or responsibilities, or who you are in the world just fall away. Your eyes may close or soften naturally. Notice that the more you focus on the sights, sounds, and smells, how your surroundings are becoming you. Absorb yourself in the otherness of this place you are in now ... Choose one element near you, or let it choose you. It could be a rock, tree, stream, animal, plant, even the breeze itself. Suspend your disbelief from the "ordinary mind" and imagine what this otherness of nature feels like. Then believe what follows ... Your breath slows even further, with perhaps a deep sigh effortlessly releasing itself. You connect easily with wellbeing, both yours and with one greater than yourself. You lose self-consciousness and willingly perceive through the aspect of nature that has chosen you. You effortlessly glide into that other as it simultaneously moves into you ... Notice how easily and pleasantly you merge.

Now you can relax even more deeply with the impressions you receive, letting your mind know in ways it doesn't normally know, your body feel in ways it may not normally feel. You'll accept only impressions, feelings, or information that have your highest interest at heart and are in service of the Divine. Let the experience be what it is ... Time can pass without notice. You are in another realm now.

When you are ready, you may breathe deeply again and gently release the thoughts and feelings of otherness while retaining enough to mull over later. Feel once again the distinctness of your own life and body ... Breathe back into yourself ... You will emerge with a greater understanding of all that is around you. As you open or refocus your eyes and see distinctly again, you'll notice the differences between you and the natural world. You will come back to yourself more connected without and within ... As you leave the private place you've visited (whether in actual or virtual reality), give thanks for your experience. As soon as possible, you could choose to journal, draw, share with a trusted friend, make music, dance, do yoga, or practice any kind of movement that draws meaning from your experience. You'll want to drink water, eat something healthy, and make sure you have returned to ordinary consciousness enough to return to ordinary life.

Come back with me now, if you will, to the trail I disappeared into right before your own experience. It is looping back toward where I think I parked my car, how many hours ago? I check the position of the sun. It has moved a bit; not as far as I feel it should have, given how far away I've been in the inner terrain. That's what altered time does to you. But in the here and now, flies are still buzzing around my head, the lupine are swaying in the breeze, and I am careening around rocks strewn across the dusty trail. I ponder as my feet propel me along. The brief encounter I have had today reminds me of the vast power of all that I have ignored. I forgive myself for retreating for months from the strength of the natural world and take heart, vowing to come back more often. As I age, I hope these absences diminish even more, so my heart can expand in kinship with all that is wild, and cyclical, and without guile. It will restore me to the best of my own natural self. It can restore you, too.

This brave way of living connected to nature, so open and so raw, challenges us. It can be difficult to sustain, but the reward is so much greater than the effort. Even if we have neglected a relationship with nature, we can return again and again to live in a naked and innocent way in the world. "Come," says Jalaluddin Rumi, the Sufi mystic, "no matter how often you have broken your vows, come, come again." To come again back to nature as friend, to renew intimate relations, to sink into the roots of worship, offers regeneration and hope.

The trail I've been padding back along to my car spits me out at the road in what turns out to have been just a short two hours. Driving back to town and re-entering the ordinary world, I find myself enlivened to magic everywhere. The buildings vibrate with presence, even the asphalt streets, the cars zooming up and down Main Street, the shopkeepers sweeping their front steps. I park and walk to my favorite lunch spot. I am seated at a table next to a young man wearing a T-shirt that says "You Belong Outdoors" who stares intently at me and asks if I've just returned from the mountains. How did he know? He said he saw it in my eyes. The mountains must have reached him through the image I was still carrying. And he was perceptive enough to notice.

It is never too late to come back to the heart of nature, to the trails that beg your remembrance or your first visit. Even if you live in the city and can only get to the mountains or the plains or the desert once a year, wherever you come most alive, you could find enough to sustain you and a vision that could change your entire life. It is never too late to return—or to begin.

15

All That Renews

Story is the most precious container of the Spirit.
—Laurens van der Post

At the close of a hot summer, I am once again breathing deep the living grounds of moose. Cedar-like leafy smells of fading summer willows and fresh water from curving streams roll through this high mountain country.

I am winding my way up mountainous roads to stay at what I have come to call "my" lovely (rented) cabin right in the midst of moose habitat. This is ripe moose country—the West Fork of the Bitterroot River, which winds into the heights beyond passable roads and flows without borders between southwest Montana and eastern Idaho.

Meandering in my open-windowed Jeep along these roads, I am possessed by the drive to become invisible, imbibing the urgent call of pine trees and forgetting myself. I transmute back to an age far older than the dirt roads that allow my vehicle to transport me to my place of renewal. I am old as the streams that envelop the rocks in ruffled whitewater passageways, the wetness slapping over me. I am cold and damp like the old stones, grown smooth from such turbulence.

Ecclesiastes teaches us that everything has its season. All things change, as I am right now. I lose who I am with every mile I travel into the sheltering forests, with every stand of trees, open meadows, and sheltered streams that have thrived so well without my presence this past year.

The land has preserved itself beyond the necessary ecological concerns, maintaining a deeper dream where even needed political activism has no hold. I know the sacred lives here. As its visitor, I resolve to find a deeper knowing beyond human concern or stewardship. Like the shamans of old, I am made an "other," blessed with knowing and a sense of long-awaited relief.

The stream beside me gurgles and whispers, and the road has several wide portions for pulling over. I shun my automobile in favor of sneaking steps and suppressed giggles into the waiting willows. I welcome the irony of becoming more alive while fading as a human. I lose my shame of our collective greed and my two-legged limitations, dropping them like old mantles that are no longer needed. Now I am "other," part of everything around me, breathing in the wind through pungent branches and staunch willow stands. Soon I will see moose. Their long, dusty brown muzzles will open deftly to chew on streamside branchings. The tall willows may almost cover their massive bodies, but I will spot one by finding a lone willow whose top branches tremble with the feeding. I tremble too, thrilled at such danger and awkward beauty so close to my own.

I only track animals; I do not hunt them. Though hunting for population control, or in some cases for food, may be warranted in certain situations and more kind than letting herds develop disease and starvation, I could not end the life of a bull moose moving sleekly across an open meadow, intent on his love of the season, preparing to make next year's calf crop. While my intellect approves of a fast bullet rather than a slow starvation, in my own heaven, neither would happen.

I can smell them whenever I get close—the ripeness of their musky bodies caked with damp and dried pond residue. Suddenly, through a natural archway of willows and a mere twenty feet from me, I see him. He faces me, regal and tall, and his massive shoulders hold his neck and heavy paddles with ease. His eyes enlarge as they take me in but stay soft and round. I stand in awe of the majesty of this bull in his prime, his stately antlers well placed below lopping ears. His sloped, defined muzzle is rounded like the edges of the state I live in, curved and gracious. I feel a rush of undeserved pride that my Montana homeland provides habitat for these magnificent creatures, nurturing and sustaining both their lives and my own.

The moose, however, starts to look agitated, begins to snort (never a good sign), and just as I am beginning a careful retreat, arcs away into the underbrush. Soon I no longer see or hear him. Still, I feel his presence; I am with kin here. There is an ineffable knowing deep in my body of the ability to survive well with such shy reserve. Like me, moose are quiet until challenged. Then they defend themselves with potential deathly attack; they can be swift and sure. They thrive despite all the threats to their habitat, despite fires and deforestation. So many other species are becoming extinct—birds and toads and insects—yet these obvious mammoths persist. This thrills me. It offers hope for the future.

I am reminded again of the happy fact that moose survival has taught me how to live alone. Through moose, I have learned how to thrive through long winters and short lovemaking sessions. I understand growing babies and losing them. Look how I can stride into each day and blend into my environment, no matter how deep the sorrow, find sustenance and renewal, and glide through change. Moose help me remember.

Recently, at a Native American elders gathering in Northern California, I heard a speaker reiterate the somewhat well-known ancient (now current) theory that all animal species have developed themselves to the ultimate of what they can do; now they are only waiting for us to perfect our human selves so we can all move on together to become truly new. I like to think so. This newness would encompass no killing or need to rule over others. All would live in harmony within and between species. My sense that there was a time when we once lived like that deepens each time I see beauty in nature and contracts each time I see suffering. Holding a place for heaven on earth, I continue to hold the vision that rather than humans conquering others (whether in relation to other humans or other life forms), our reason for living becomes co-operative in a mutually agreeable situation. It's akin to world peace: a worthy effort and an ultimate goal.

Moose provide an ongoing, welcome mystery that lingers long after their disappearance. It is this mystery that calls me from my own seasons of despair. It is what pulls me to take one more trip to find them, to get close enough to hear my heart beating loud in my ears as they listen for my foolish, eager approach.

It is nearly sunset as I arrive at my cabin in the Bitterroot Mountains. My friends, who manage the ranch, are in town on errands; they simply leave the cabin unlocked for me. Our reunion will happen tomorrow. As I drive into the far edge of the meadow with my windows down, I breathe in the eucalyptus-like musty smell of autumn leaves. It's fall breeding season for both elk and moose, and I know I will not sleep well. I can feel the excitement of moose everywhere. Unpacking my Jeep in the fading light, I can barely make out the forms of a healthy young cow and first-season calf heaving out of the pond halfway down the meadow. I wiggle with the thrill but stay close to the cabin, knowing that in the time I'd take to approach them, they would be gone. They shake off water and quickly depart. Under the setting sun, I see the indistinct winding trails they have cut through green willows and can barely make out their tracks in the sand by the river's edge. Moose droppings are close by the streambeds and bedding places. I am alive in moose habitat, their very living space! Even when I am indoors throughout the night, I awaken to the sound of woofs, the sure long strides, the soft and rhythmic thudding on marsh-meadows, the crackling of branches. Never sure where my dreaming leaves off and earth-time begins, I travel between the worlds while I toss and wait for daylight.

Early morning reveals the open expanse of meadow and ponds. While dressing for the outdoors, I am suddenly called to the kitchen window by the kind of knowing that says "now," and there he is, within ten feet of my cabin: a marvelous, sleek, deep wet chocolate-brown bull with highlights of amber red. He is in full rut, ambling adroitly past me, his eyes and ears intent upon the willows at the south side of the meadow. The female and her calf I'd seen on my way in must be tucked away in those thickets. As I slip into boots and a jacket and head out the back door, he never even glances back at me, though I am sure he is aware of my presence. Using every bit of restraint I possess and aware of my human limitations, I keep a respectful distance.

I am watching the moose's ears since, like a horse's, they tell me everything that is going on around them. I watch how he holds his head so I'll know if he considers me friend or foe, familiar or strange. This knowledge may help keep me safe. Then I pray, use my best judgment, cross the meadow, and disappear after him right into the waiting willows.

16

The War Within

We used to wonder where war lived, what it was that made it so vile. And now we realize that we know where it lives, that it is inside ourselves.
—Albert Camus

Summer is in her early glory, and I am once again tramping across old bridges in southwest Montana that have seen years of water pass below them. I navigate large willows and cross marshy stream bottoms quickly, picking my way to avoid hopeless bogs. Living here for twenty years has taught me how not to get my feet wet with the resulting nasty blisters. Then I spy them: a cow moose and her calf adeptly trotting around a bend in the stream. The mother stops to look back at me and blow a contemptuous warning through her nose. I am thrilled and nod my understanding to her, carefully backing up a few steps to let her know I got her point.

I sigh and sit down a short way off the trail with my back to a large conifer as the moose ambles slowly upstream. The moose I've just been corrected by is not at war within herself. She will make war on me if I ignore her boundaries, but she is not expressing inner conflict. She evidences ease and contentment. On this perfect summer day, however, I am battling insecurities and am in the midst of strife within. What does she have that I do not?

Perhaps it's what she doesn't have. Most likely she doesn't have the self-reflective capacity that humans do. Though our capacity to self-reflect and utilize our complex reasoning systems seem necessary to solve conflict, perhaps our very ability to reason creates the need for self-reflection. While self-reflection gifts us with the ability to be conscious, to appreciate nature, others, and life itself, this same gift can lead to neurosis and great inner turmoil. I can feel angst, confusion, self-absorption, happiness, sadness, and confidence all at once. I never see evidence of this in moose, or any animals, unless they have been treated poorly by humans!

I am self-reflecting today about a comment recently made by a colleague. She was disparaging another who was living alone, saying, "No wonder; she's just so irritating." Like a good neurotic, of course I took it personally. She must really be talking about me. Yet later she said, "My husband will probably leave me one of these days because I'm so difficult." Oh, not about me after all.

She had projected her own fear of being rejected onto someone else. And I projected my fear of being inadequate by taking her comments to heart. When we see our part in any conflict, whether external or internal, we can draw back the curtain of projection that sees the other (or another part of ourselves) as having all the faults and us as having none, or vice versa. As we do so, we see more clearly those "demons" within. I love the old comic book character Pogo's insightful remark, "We have seen the enemy and it is us." He has discovered the truth of our psyche's makeup. When we discover the true source of true aggression to be our own self-judging, we begin to truly take responsibility for ourselves. Other people or situations merely trigger, or serve as mirrors, for that which is yet undone and unloved within. The problem lies within us. Resolution is the challenge.

My best way of making peace within is simply to spend time in nature. Particularly when I am in the company of moose, I find a great capacity to simply accept whatever I am ill at ease about. I take in the presence of a moose wading effortlessly through a rock-filled stream as a template for how to pick my own way through that which bothers me. Like moose, I too have innate capacity to adeptly wade through my life. By watching them, I realize how I can choose balance over imbalance, skill over awkwardness. Then issues either resolve or I am able to treat them and myself with compassion while they are working themselves out.

When we cannot make peace within, we war without. War is the ultimate projection and most primitive reaction humans could have; it shows a serious and deadly lack of imagination. Even years later, my thoughts are never far from the aging yet ageless events of 9/11 or the ongoing Middle East wars, though they are only samples of the many worldwide losses over the years and harbingers of wars yet to come. The grief of those who remain behind and the very idea of widespread chemical warfare stops my breath. Yet on a clear summer morning, walking adeptly to avoid the mud at my feet, I am also aware of how in the United States we are challenged on our own soil to avoid the bogs of reactionary thinking and victorious victimhood. "The Home of the Brave" has become "The Home of the Self-Righteous."

We seek the enemy abroad; I try to understand the exigencies of this. But many US citizens never question the assumption that we are all good and "they" are all bad. With this attitude, as Sam Keen points out in his book *Faces of the Enemy*, we are missing a unique opportunity to learn from and reexamine our policies through the lens of our enemies as well as friends abroad. The degree to which we elevate our own righteousness is the degree to which all that is dark in ourselves becomes repressed and denied.

Other cultures often see our national shadow better than we do. A Turkish woman visiting our country I met stated, "The United States doesn't understand how it is seen by most foreign nations. We see you as adolescents misusing power in the guise of benevolence, but in reality very controlling and self-seeking." Native Americans would say that we often do not act like "a good animal," who would act only to protect, not to aggress. Natives tell European-Caucasians that we are the erring younger brother exploiting ill-used strength without the wisdom to wield it. Even the Bible, long-used in American defense, asks how we can take out the speck in another's eye without first taking out the log in our own. In these troubled times, we have a rare opportunity to see our collective shadow and to truly grieve and change our selfish ways. Only when we have begun to accept our own faults and forgive ourselves will we be able to deal with outer circumstance with more alacrity. Only then will we begin to be "good animals."

Moose Medicine can help all of us learn how to make peace with the enemy within. Moose are large and potentially very dangerous, but only when unreasonably bothered. They hold no grudges, because they teach each other to respect boundaries, and they retain that memory. They offer a sense of self-acceptance and ego-approval within the consciousness of a sentient spirit. Native tribes believe this too: moose represent the medicine of thinking well of ourselves within proper ego boundaries. They remind us of the importance of congratulating ourselves for a job well done. Jamie Sams, who like myself is an honorary member of the Wolf Clan of the Seneca Nation, writes about several animal totems in her book *Medicine Cards: The Discovery of Power Through the Ways of Animals*. She explains that Moose Medicine people know when to use the gentleness of deer (moose are related to the deer species) and when to stamp like buffalo. We also will know when to keep our egos in check and when to listen to others. Another author, Ted Andrews, speaks through his Animal Cards of the moose's great deftness and speed in negotiating difficult territory. Moose are believed to offer spiritual discernment, incredible strength, and wisdom.

We do not have to be overtaken by darkness when we recognize our own less-than-lovely aspects and work with them rather than against them to heal ourselves. In my private practice as a body-mind-spirit therapist, I teach an informative system called "Voice Dialogue," where the clients identify various parts of themselves that are present in a conflict and then give each part a voice. Each part is treated as an actor with its own script. Parts of the self are identified, and I interview them, asking about their purpose in that person's life. Even unappealing parts usually want to be loved, or at least appreciated, and when questioned resoundingly report that they originally developed out of a basic good intention, even if they learned to express it poorly. When we listen to these parts, respect them, set any needed boundaries, and educate each part as to the person's current needs, they harmonize. Because we are seeking to understand, not reject, we feel a great sense of relief as a result. We discover the truth of the title of Dawna Markova's groundbreaking book *No Enemies Within*. As she reminds us, our shadow sides can live side by side with our whole selves, and we are the richer for it.

Nature continually deals with its own shadow of decay and our effects of pollution upon it, restoring and rebalancing itself all the time. The earth is still birthing and dying, providing seasons of light and dark, bringing heat and cold, rain and sun. In spite of the wars and resulting devastation that we create, the earth itself is still lovely. If I forget this and fail to seek the intimate experience of woods, mountains, lakes, and streams, I am truly lost.

The moose I love amble slowly upstream, dipping in cold waters to reach nourishing streamside fronds. Their pungent smell reaches my nostrils, and it is familiar, not unpleasant. I watch them in awe and then return home to sobering waters in my country and abroad. May we learn to fare as well as these wild creatures, receive our lessons, and make peace from the war within.

17

No Longer a Poultice

Great pain, when it is honored from the heart, opens into great understanding.
—Jack Kornfield

During my young adult life, the mountains provided solace to ease my emotional wounds from a troubled upbringing and what became an unhappy marriage. Nature offered a poultice: "Look, see Eagle flying just above you," "Smell the damp moss at the base of this pungent cedar tree," "Here, enjoy the surprises around every small bend and turn: a deer grazing, a coyote den," and "Ah, this stream has stories to tell. Listen." This secondary solace was the attempt to heal human wounding with another source. But secondary solace always falls short of complete healing. As a teacher of mine explained, we must heal our wounding through the same vehicle of the wound itself. So if our wounds came from a human, we do best to heal them through humans, but safe and loving ones the second time around. And that is what I found—a good therapist and three powerful healers who helped me forgive others and myself. All the while, I kept interspersing demanding psychological work with the salve of time in nature.

For a time, finding simple joy in hiking through the mountains had sustained me, helping me better attend to the necessary human tasks: paying bills, keeping up a home, and doing varied work for income. Wandering trails, winding through thick stands of trees, and discovering seldom-seen mountain lakes and waterfalls gifted me with the will to stay on, to find a way to be inspired by and related to everything. I am among those who know in every cell of my body what it is to *be* a wildflower, a stone, a deer, and an elephant's ear. In these unexpected moments, perhaps invited by a stilled mind, human sense would be quieted while "otherness" suffused awareness. I know that the flower feels its own luminosity from within, the soft petals an extension of its own feeling body. Stones carry low vibrations necessary to the rhythms and timing of all earth processes, knowledge I have also felt in my own body. From being in the essence of a deer, I know that they quiver from the center of their heart every moment of their lives. The elephant's ear pulses with a thousand rivers of membranes, each connecting to a deep memory, taking in each new sound to add to its ceaseless collection. And in more ordinary moments, I have simply looked up into the night sky and watched the stars travel across the heavens, appreciating a benign god who must have created all this beauty to sustain us.

Yet the days before and following a very difficult and long-considered divorce and the resulting death of my dreams of an intact, happy family began to haunt me. Still, my work as a healer was growing. Then, suddenly, everything began to close down. One dear friend each year seemed to move out of my life. My two other businesses began to fail. My childless years were mocked by the onset of menopause, and hot flashes with restless legs made me want to crawl out of my skin. I kept grieving for the adopted children we had tried so hard to help but who had had to return to treatment homes. Somewhere in that darkening cavern, I simply lost interest in work. "When continued effort has no yield, discontinue effort," became my mantra. But as I stopped the effort to feel better, I caved in to despair. Depression moved in like a greedy fog, dampening my bones with untended grief and mourning.

Somehow, I was fortunate enough to have found a mentor who was able to accompany me at least to the edges of my dark passage. I also discovered a book, *The Soul in Grief*, by Robert Romanyshyn, that spoke to my feelings on every page. He wrote with pained accuracy how shortly after his wife's sudden death, well-meaning friends told him to "forget it" and "get on with life." He continued to fall into a dark well. He grieved as I did. I mourned the birth children I never had and the adopted ones who did not bond well. He had a final death; I was adjusting to a living one. The story of all his dark nights was also mine, and the long time it took him to "come back" mine also.

Extended, untended sorrow can invite thoughts of suicide, which I think is actually a dark temptation to keep following that which was lost. I was sickened with hopelessness, disappointments, and sorrows that woke me at night and haunted me during the day. My own family disowned me for divorcing, as did all of our sixteen couple friends whom I had nurtured and drawn together for frequent dinners at our home. I left our beautiful country house for a small, dark apartment in town. His income increased, and I had none, as we had agreed I would not work outside the home in order to raise the children, the ones who were failing to attach to us. At the time, I did not, as Jack Kornfeld wrote, find I could honor great pain, which might then "open into great understanding." The deep disappointment I felt made sense, but my heart was inconsolable and I found no mental relief that would put loss into context.

The lens of wounding can magnify faults—both private and public weaknesses. Even as I struggled with my own very imperfect ways of dealing with loss, through the unconsciousness of food, alcohol, and sexual encounters, I found myself reflecting on older tribal societies. They seemed to live in such harmony with nature and derived such communal support from it. My bones shuddered to feel the separateness of our species now. My past numinous experiences with nature were reminding me that I could know what it was like to live as one. I felt such a time in my bones, maybe before this life, when I must have been part of an older and wiser society, living in connection with all around me. I sorely missed that way of being in my present life. I was uncomfortably aware of my isolation from others and theirs from me, and I felt the ultimate communal sorrow of a race gone bad, unable to pull itself or others back from inevitable destruction.

As the days of my dead personal dreams continued to decay, I began to sink into a blank, colorless nothingness. It went beyond clinical depression. I unwittingly entered into a place the sages call "the void": there is no place to go, no place that heals, no gods or goddesses, no Mommy and Daddy to heal wounds. The big picture was totally lost as the small picture of my life loomed large, even in its atrophy. My "feeling body" was convinced that I would never get out. I could only breathe while feeling that I was dying, only watch the days pass with no thought, or feeling, or sense of anything but the vague passing of time.

Although I had been moving into becoming a healer, now I could not even remember or access what had healed me in the past. In the void, I could only wait, forming the first whisper of surrender. I slowly realized I would have to release my sense of being victimized by the void in order to take the active stance of acceptance. The hardest point came when I was *almost* at the threshold of letting all my desires go, all my imagined controls, all the ways I'd been busy trying to keep my life from getting any worse. That is the worst place to be, because at that moment, I began to see the lightness of the other side and all the joy I'd been missing while lost. And that was something to grieve.

In the void, to sit in nothingness is all you can do. It is a time to experience the harsh cold of winter and to endure. During this time, nature was unable to provide her familiar poultice, and I felt utterly abandoned. I was, however, beginning to learn to be present to my own pain and reality. Finally, I gave up hope and just surrendered. "Help me live this day, this moment, just as it is, with no complaint, no demand, and no expectation," became my prayer. I lived this way for several months.

Then, without herald or fanfare, the deep void simply ended.

Bit by bit I began to come back to life, to forgive others and myself, to feel the sun on my face, and to know the goodness of waking up in the morning. I began to notice other people smiling and the beauty all around me. My outer life had not changed. I simply began to accept being alive on life's terms. And I opened to other humans more, no longer hiding in nature.

I remembered that while first going into the void, I had felt my spirit familiars and ancestors benignly watching from an enlarged circle they had stretched around me. After the void, their circle grew closer, and I could reach out and touch them on the spirit planes. I embraced them, prayed, sang, and laughed once again. My life re-created itself. I developed new friends, deepened my soulful career, and moved on. I even got to be at least partially accepted as a mother by the youngest of our three children, forming a bond that began to look promising.

Since those dark times, I have often looked up from the earth and prayed into the stars' nightly travel to a creator I believe wants to sustain us. I have also read many sage accounts of others who have gone through this same void. I wish I'd known about it beforehand; perhaps it could have prepared me. Though it would not likely have changed the duration, maybe it would have eased some of the angst. Perhaps this account will better prepare you in case someday you find yourself careening headlong into the void.

On the other side of the void, life once again offers so much relationship to self and others. We relate to others of our species with broader understanding and less judgment. We interact more fully with the rest of the world, wild animals and all, knowing our interspecies connection. Invited by the stilled mind, we can more easily suspend our own human senses while "otherness" suffuses our inner awareness. We can experience other life forms in a way that fills us with inspiration, amazement, and understanding.

In the outer world, I once again returned to wandering trails and winding through thick stands of trees. I now find that I can better work through whatever troubles me and find healing refreshment through mountain lakes and waterfalls. I can also find safe and loving humans to help me remember healing tools when I get my psychological ropes tied in knots. I can be inspired by and related to everything. All natural elements, humans included, along with those life forms modern science calls inanimate, have stories to offer. Stones offer wisdom, and moose allow me to crawl inside their skin and look out through their eyes.

Those eyes take in a steady stream of consciousness, at one with their environment, standing securely in the midst of rolling waters. When human seasons move from the winter of a void to the fecundity of spring, nature offers itself as poultice and a soulful transformation. When your time arrives for the void, may you breathe deeply and know yourself in the midst of your own trembling. May you learn when it is time to surrender and when it is time to find good human help. May you travel well. And when it is your turn to return from the void, may you come back with your own form of Moose Medicine. May your heart, with all its pain, open to the Great Mystery and be sustained by it.

18

Whose Greed?

I am interested in the way a man looks at a given landscape and takes possession of it in his blood and brain ... I believe it is possible to formulate an ethical idea of the land—a notion of what it is and must be in our daily lives.

—N. Scott Momaday, Kiowa novelist

My eyes are sore from squinting at the new roads being bulldozed on a lovely slope of land that cascades down from the sheltering Bridger Mountains. The roads crisscross a hillside where in winter elk range freely, and year-round the once-pristine thousand acres support deer and mountain lion. I had hoped—and wrongly assumed—that the land was in public or protected ownership. But the neighbors tell me that it is private land once owned by a rancher and used for grazing, now sold for a corporate retreat center that includes a large barn, two huge houses, and numerous scattered outbuildings. The unwelcome new roads cut into my mind and churn up what was once tranquil, fertile viewing space where my heart breathed deeply to watch elk traverse the terrain. These roads have begun to forever change my ease in relating to open space, to freedom, and to places protected from human encroachment.

Humans tend to love open space, perhaps because we get tied up in such knots in the cramped quarters of our own minds. We love shared open space that belongs to everyone and everything. At the same time, caught in the convincing lie of materialism, we all want our own piece of the pie. When it comes to land, this personal quest could be for one acre or a thousand acres. In the United States, we worry about not having enough personal space and how much "enough" might be. Escalating land prices relegate beautiful country to the rich and leave overcrowded cities to the poor. In my shadow-self moments, I judge our greed and ignorance, damning the aggressive landowners, subdividers, and developers who directly participate in the demise of the sacred.

I ache for the animals, whose shy and retiring natures will not allow them to continue to thrive here in the vanishing wilds, even in Montana. I grieve for the elk who have lost habitat and been forced farther up and onto steeper slopes with less grass for grazing. I worry that they may suffer hunger and disease just so certain humans can have lovely views of the valley below. Lands such as these are advertised in real estate brochures as "elk winter range and birthing grounds," boasting "rich wildlife," yet are "vehicle accessible." These glossy ads tout minimum development as desirable and supposedly achieve it, as though elk wouldn't mind the constant hammering and concrete pouring and traffic for years while a "spacious" subdivision is forming. The new homeowners bring along their family dogs, allowing them free rein of the unfenced homesites, as though elk would feel safe to continue bedding down and having their young anywhere near an area with these close descendants of wolves.

People to whom I complain about this encroachment often agree and nod their heads, but they uniformly say, "You can't stop progress." I have begun to answer, "Yes, you can. We must." We can lend our political voices to creating master plans for all growing cities that value open space and wiser use of land through such dedicated groups as the Rocky Mountain Elk Foundation. We can also control our burgeoning population. We can have fewer children, not only for the sake of our own diminishing quality of life on a ravished and polluted planet, but for the other creatures of the earth and the overused landforms. And we can wrestle with our own personal greed to own vast stretches of land that compromise wildlife habitat. We owe it to all things to stop this madness.

When I suggest such ideas, people around me pull back, squint their eyes, and cave into themselves. If I rail on, saying that we must keep more protected land to survive, I sooner or later also hear my own greedy anxiety hiding behind my righteousness. "Wait!" it cries. "What about me? What about my own ardent desire to live on acres of private ground with fine views and streams and undisturbed nature?"

My shadow-self, which has projected dislike onto the rich developers, also lives in me. I, too, would like a fine country home with no "white noise" from cities or agriculture, no power lines messing with my own electric body, no other humans nearby, no reminders that the whole world is not my personal paradise. If I could just have my forty or one hundred or one thousand acres of mountain land where the elk have been for years, certainly *I* wouldn't disturb them! Except with all my money, maybe I'd build a retreat center for more people to come in and enjoy the lack of development. But then maybe I'd need to sell more of those lower portions of my own land to pay the taxes if my business wasn't going well or if I just wanted to have more cash for that yacht for island getaways, or, better yet, more pristine acreage maybe in a different state. If I had the funding sources that these new landowners and developers have, my own greedy self might do just that.

I desire to live deep in nature and be soothed by her voice. To be surrounded by streams, and willows, and forested trails suits me fine. I would love to live in a setting frequented by moose. I can't get enough moose sightings, grabbing up all the experience my hungry little soul can hold. Greed quite clearly lives in me, as I turn a jealous eye to the acreage being developed above my small country subdivision. Though I will move into town soon, for now I am still living close to the mountains who have become, as Alice Walker writes, "my familiars."

I try to justify my anger. Our one-road country lane seems less of a grievance, since it's on former farmland; the acreage above sits on pristine wooded slopes. Viewing the spreading uphill roads and rising buildings from my small backyard, I complain with the neighbors against the developer's poor use of the land. I live daily with this dilemma, stuck between an urgency to protect the land and the desire to afford my own little piece of it.

I don't know how to resolve this yet or how to become the selfless person I believe would sacrifice personal pleasure for the common good. I only know that for now I am willing to let these contradictory urges live in me. Sages have claimed that holding the tension of opposites is what will eventually help us to coalesce them, bringing about global unity and ultimate nirvana. They remind us that when we truly understand that we are all one, we will care for every living being as we would ourselves. I like to keep that in mind while I face my very humanly imperfect battles in my own backyard.

19

All on the Same Rope

Learning is the very essence of humility, learning from everything and everybody. There is no hierarchy in learning.
—Krishnamurti

"Competition," says the pageant director, who decides to preach to me, "is a *must* to succeed in society. This one," she continues, pointing to a photo of a film star, "she's higher up on the rope than I am, but I'm higher than he is [pointing out the window to a construction worker], down there."

I shake my head in disbelief and ask, "How is it we're all on the same rope?"

My indignation about competitiveness is rivaled only by my drive to be the best at disemboweling it. I recognize this as my shadow nature, even though I truly believe that our evolving path as humans is to change our focus from competition to co-operation. In the twenty-first century, from New Age groups to gatherings of international diplomats, many social, political, and spiritual discussions center around finding ways to assist each other to be equals on different ropes, so we respect diversity while honoring our basic unity. This is the principle of cooperation, not competition.

Competition and survival of the fittest still seems to be the primary driver in the natural world, with much to be said for how it has sleeked out the best and most fit animals and plants in the right locations. The reason that we as humans must embrace more cooperation, however, is clear in relation to our ecosphere. If we want to protect our environment—animals, plants, air, and water—we have to cooperate with the very elements that are trying to coexist with us. As long ago as the thirteenth century, St. Francis of Assisi posited that we must embrace "a democracy of creatures," where none is more important than the next. Today, rather than encroaching on grazing grounds and decimating rainforest habitats, we must learn to limit our population growth and reduce our toxic products. The Sierra Club, designed to "promote the responsible use of the earth's ecosystems and resources," has chapters nationwide dealing with just such local, regional, and state issues. The Greater Yellowstone Coalition, which protects the lands, waters, and wildlife of the Yellowstone ecosystem, also seeks to find ways of protecting public land with minimum intervention. It seeks a healthy interaction, not a competition for resources and space that will crowd out the needs of the many to accommodate the desires of the few. Competition has brought us beyond the brink of world disaster, and we are now living in the midst of the messes we have made. Cooperation is critical if we are to halt the onslaught of the planetary damage we perpetrate daily.

I can feel outraged about these issues publically, but the shadow side of my personality (the parts of my personality or actions I don't tend to own as mine, whether positive or negative) contains my codependent self, which wants everyone to be happy, everyone to be pleased, and everything to be nice. Cooperation is nice; competition can be ruthless. Another face of my shadow side contains the urge to compete and be the best at what I do. The extent to which I refuse to see this ruthlessness in myself may also be the extent to which I avoid or despise competition. If I hate competition, I am outwardly denying my competitive nature; on the other hand, if I thrive exclusively on competition, I outwardly deny my cooperative side. Wild animals cooperate more easily when there is enough food and territory to go around, and so do we.

Scarcity breeds human fear, and fear of "not enough" drives competition. On the psychological level, this fear can take the form of constant doing and an incessant ego drive to achieve. When is it we ever have achieved enough? A poem I wrote reads:

> She never felt she had enough, did enough, mattered enough
> Until one day she disappeared and was never found again
> Because of course, she was not enough.

Like animals, we compete to survive. But we go beyond survival; we continue to compete to gratify egos and prove ourselves "better" than others. Although many of our quality-of-life improvements and lifesaving scientific discoveries have come as a result of this urge to succeed, we have also paid a price. We have overridden our natural interconnection, which the animal world still possesses. Animals compete without vice, only out of necessity; in contrast, humans are wantonly cruel to each other as we struggle to become the best or to acquire the most.

One way of considering the "competition vs. cooperation" problem is to look at the current patriarchy, the masculine approach that's in charge both in men and women, though primarily still led by men. Patriarchy at its best would breed order, excellence, and bravery. At its worst it breeds chaos, misuse of power, and war. The matriarchy from ages ago at its best bred intuitive knowing, compassion, and beauty. At its worst it invited unchecked rage, betrayal, and heartlessness. So now, with the current patriarchy imploding and our leading edge of consciousness seeking to truly balance the best of these masculine and feminine qualities, how can we mitigate our own overly masculine competitiveness?

I find nature to be a solace for this need to achieve. It helps me rebalance and experience rest and serenity. When my senses are filled by the natural world, my self-worth is no longer based on achievement, and I don't need to know all the answers. As the poet Rainer Maria Rilke wrote, sometimes we can "live the questions" and "perhaps gradually live into the answers." Moose remind me of this, simply and intuitively filling me with great amazement, and wonder, and a feeling of perfect peace. Why I feel such depths when I gaze at these animals, I do not know. I only know I do not feel competition when in their presence; I feel the desire for cooperation.

Competitiveness does breed a kind of order, which follows the initial chaos and puts everything in its place. Peace within herds of buffalo, for example, exists because each animal, usually through conflict, has learned its place in the herd (or on the rope, if you will). They usually inflict minimum wounding and seldom truly hurt each other; on the other hand, we humans have a horrendous history of mutilating self and other. However, we also possess the drive as a species to create a more mutual way of ordering our own society through compassion. Since we're at the top of the food chain, we need to apply sentience to our care of each other and of all life. We need to, as Gandhi said, "be the change we want to see."

My growing belief that all other forms of nature are already evolved and waiting for us to do the same engenders hope for more cooperation than competition. Maybe when humans evolve enough, all of creation will then morph into a new heaven and earth that does not need to compete for anything. This vision, shared by many, believes in a future possibility where nothing preys upon anything else and all live in perpetual peace. Meanwhile, I battle right along with my species as we struggle to be the best, or worst, we can be.

I know that my still all-too-reptilian human self can get lost in competition. When I do so, I have fallen into unconscious fear. The patriarchal manifesto (in men and women alike) in my head says, "You must succeed at all costs. If you don't achieve you'll be worthless, vulnerable, and weak. Step over others to get *yours*."

I know that some competition is still necessary at this time on earth, yet I seek to keep evolving my understanding about why it is needed and when. I am better at doing so than I used to be; I do not fail to appreciate the irony of that statement. Meanwhile, my cooperative and more feminine self thrives on nature and builds inspiration from time spent peacefully outdoors. I think I'd better return now to the nearby moose habitat of rivers and streams and let the heat from all the competitive angst that has become activated in me flow downstream. I'll just breathe into the cooling late afternoon air and feel the grass beneath my feet.

Competition has too often blinded us to the path of cooperation. Surely we will find our way through. We must. With enough peaceful centering and conscious living, we just may.

20

Arid Passageways

A fine wind is blowing the new direction of Time.
If only I let it bear me, carry me.
—D. H. Lawrence

Wind dries parched soil under my feet like a cracked canvas. Those same winds have blown me far south of my Montana home to the Arizona desert. I have returned to the southern chain of the Rocky Mountains in Tucson to see if I can find any traces of my younger self who visited this verdant landscape some years earlier. I find the Sonoran desert still alive with wrens and coyote, javelina (wild pigs), and rare blooming cactus. At one time, my own blooming had been rare, and beautiful. Yet now I have aged. Can I retrieve that freer, sensual self? I scratch my fifty-something skin, marveling at my body's history. My memories undulate, stark and real, like stretches of crusty red desert. The children I had. The children I didn't have. The men I was with whom I didn't love. The one I was smart enough to love. Those moist edges of my life story lie deep underground now, with only the relentless wind to accompany me. My body's furnace matches the one-hundred-degree days, cooling little at night. Yet somehow I take comfort in being in this desert that knows me, a spot drier than I am now or will ever be. My own arid passageways have found a dusty home.

The habitat for arid creatures of the desert stretches out in dry expanse. I marvel at how the required territory for moose is so vastly different. They require slosh and wet, fecund fronds of greenery to dangle from their antlers and mush around in their mouths like cows chewing their cud. They slurp through river bottoms and muddy shores replete with insects and sheltering trees. This was the habitat of my body in its early years. I was juicy, ripe, and fecund. I reveled in my watery being and sloshed through many nourishing adventures. Though I love the memory of those more fluid days, now my body has *become* the desert in all her starkness.

Women in midlife know about arid passageways. Our bodies change with inconvenient sweats and bilateral jumps of emotion. Unwelcome lapses of memory embarrass and yet convince us to develop a more intuitive and less didactic way of thinking. Men do not generally have such dramatic midlife signals, so their own crises of thought or emotion can take on a more startling initiation ("Who knew he would do that?" and "I can't imagine why …").

Western society ignores or minimizes most rites of passage. From my years of work with people in transition, I am convinced that becoming conscious of all the nuances of whatever change is brewing serves us well. When a client becomes aware of the struggle or change she is facing, her psyche responds positively to the attention. The psyche can then clarify what's needed and hopefully get what it needs. For example, if at midlife a woman will review her personal history and finish some necessary grieving, she may move through this time with grace instead of acting out. If she refuses her opportunity, she may evidence indicators that she has not progressed through this rite of passage: she may begin to incessantly party with a younger crowd, dress in younger clothes, have extensive plastic surgery, or go twittering about like a young girl. This is all because she has not honored her wrinkles as a mark of life's experience, and no one has stopped to ask her, "What have you learned from your years?" Or she acts out like the unhappy Grail King in the Arthurian legend because no one has asked her, "What ails thee?"

When no one is asking us this question, we must ask it for ourselves. The gifts of the resulting greater consciousness are many. We seek to plumb the caverns of our own hearts and become the dedicated friend to ourselves we always wanted to be. We learn self-forgiveness and reprioritize thoughts and activity. We allow relationships to change as needed with more ease. We may become more trusting of our intuition and more introspective. Our lives become a journey of adventure and discovery, a recognition that indeed we have been on a quest for our own femininity. As authors Jean Shinoda Bolen and Dan Brown have so aptly declared, this journey is guided by the sacred feminine. Both authors also agree that the feminine is present and asking for attention in both men and women, just as the masculine is a force in both genders too. My own CD *The Return of the Sacred Feminine* records women in midlife declaring the truths of their own journeys and offers ways for both men and women to self-discover what is stirring in their own inner feminine and masculine landscape.

In our Western youth-oriented and materialistic society, there are few motivators to develop spirituality, to "put a foot on the other side," to journey to invisible destinations, or to build a relationship with the Great All. As we age, however, it just makes sense that we would be better served to get to know our approaching destination: death itself and that which lies beyond the experience of the body.

To breathe deep in midlife is to feel dryness on our tongues and know how our own clay bodies are turning to dust.

If we refuse to expand our thoughts to what comes next, our lives can become withered caricatures serving no one, not even ourselves. Or if we bury ourselves in busyness, we lose the opportunity to become deeper, more soulful beings by accompanying ourselves into a place of barrenness. We women know this empty place waits for us—physically, mentally, and emotionally. Ironically, this place is full of power and wisdom. If we can accept the now-empty womb and embrace the physical release of monthly cycling, then we can turn our eyes inward toward the rhythms of our own desert and learn to embrace the landscape.

If a woman in midlife can be present to her own aridity, she can dwell in the truth of her passage and stay there until the psyche's landscape changes of its own accord. She may alternately love and hate all the changes life brings, feeling them viscerally as both blessings and curses. Whether in a moist high country river setting or the sweeping desert climate, we live most fully when we recognize and accept whichever place we find ourselves, not leaving before we have learned all it has to teach, both on the physical and metaphorical levels.

In my own midlife, I have found that by persevering through physical changes, younger parts of my life that needed to dry up have desiccated and blown away in the wind. Certain ways of looking at life and demands I made in wanting life to turn out a specific way are now useless to me, and I bless and release them on the hot evening breeze. But like any good desert plant, I also notice I am sprouting a few barbed parts—cactus stickers that can poke those who have failed to use caution. When needed, I apologize for untactful words, but not for myself. Like ancient saguaro cacti, which only grow their unique and fascinating arms over many years, I have earned my interesting features and rugged beauty. I store all I need deep in my roots, including the water that nourishes me through this dry season. This also helps me flower and attract just the right species of bird to appreciate my rare blooming, as well as the right partner to admire my own uplifted arms, even if the flesh sags a bit.

Tucson turned out to be just the right medicine. While there, I explored the lovely Sabino Canyon, cavorting in deep sandstone pools carved by water and wind, and strolled among brother souls in the bodies of my marvelous Saguaro friends. I cried a little for lost loves and laughed a lot, deep belly laughs that came from lessons well-learned. Yet the willowed streams of moose country eventually called me North again. Once back home in Montana, I found my old topographic map and let my finger trace the entire Rocky Mountains' winding north-south undulations, lingering over the places on this length of mystery I know. I trust that for eons I have belonged to the entire chain of the Rocky Mountains, through all my passageways, from boggy willows housing adept moose to dry deserts sporting wiggly javelina. Surely this land, which has helped me know myself in so many astounding ways, will shelter my dry bones even when my spirit has flown.

21
The Nature of Time

The most beautiful understanding in the world is that of the mysterious.
—Albert Einstein

A cooling summer breeze blows the stars in for another Montana night. I am sipping the evening air by the stream that runs the length of my small acreage. It forms a small ecosystem foreign to Montana's normal dry climate; the water and its muddy shores encourage lilies, butterflies, willows, and even crickets who whine with sharp, tinny voices. Though my surroundings should carry peace, when I forget midlife teachings, instead the seemingly random timing of the crickets' chirps simply makes each moment an annoying cacophony. As they screech on, they amplify my past regrets, present anxieties, and blank future, which all convene in a tight packet of suspended time.

Time. It's that one "other" we feel we can stretch or condense, expand or contract, depending on situation and attitude. Time, that mysterious force we can tease, cajole, insist upon, play with, work with, and work against. Time is neither a lover nor a hater. It is the ever-present keeper of life. It shapes my days, and it culled short the life of the birds that died of starvation in my yard last winter. It cut me short of having my own birth children. Time is a phantom, though it holds the capacity to become friend or foe. In its trickster function, as quantum physics is attempting to explain to us, it fools us into thinking it is an acquaintance with whom we could have a reliably good *time*.

Time reigns as master of life here on earth in popular perception—and possibly of life in all galaxies. But rather than dwelling on the philosophical anomalies of time and timelessness, I'd rather work with the concept as it has become embedded in our psyches. It contains light and dark for us; it forms a reliable structure of days, nights, and years, yet can also be an unwelcome harbinger of change, the cloaked invisible that beckons us on, ready or not. It holds us accountable yet never has to be accountable itself. I'd like to live in the beauty of simplicity to accept all of life in time's parameters. Perhaps that's why I've spent so much time outdoors, in nature, and especially with my beloved moose. The natural world runs on its own time, in its own seasons, in a reasonable manner and with understandable gait. It separates me from the relentless daily tick and turn of the clock's hands.

Moose, who live on their own time, continually cause me to wonder at the creativity of the universe. Like all animals in the wild, moose do not spend time fighting the reality of their restrictions; they just take care of themselves instinctively and accept what comes their way. That's not to say that animals or plants necessarily like all the situations in which they find themselves. Often depression or death takes them too, when time has created too much hell (captivity, physical or emotional suffering), or when, for whatever reason, it is their time to go. The animal population seems to live in a kind of harmony with time. They are masters at living in the Great Mystery.

Only humans rail against the natural order of the passing days. We seem to have an arrogant capacity to challenge time, argue with it, attempt to cajole it, and imagine we can control it. We splice genes, invent aging remedies, deny midlife passages, and attempt to deny death. Of course, time always has the last laugh.

Clichés about time arise from both our cooperative and our adversarial relationship to it. "I had a great *time*," "I'm in love this *time*," "I can get that done on *time*," all express positive outcomes in relation to this constant partner. On the other hand, we have, "*Time*'s up," "I ran out of *time*," "I had a horrible *time*," "The hands of *time*" (we personify it so much), and culturally biased terms like "Indian *time*" can all convey negative associations. And, of course, time is the executive director of our ultimate foe—Death.

At important junctures in our lives, however, time itself can feel superfluous, even suspended, when we experience a deep psychological or spiritual passageway. When your life seems to grind to a halt and you see yourself as outside the influence of past, present, or future, a timelessness ensues that ironically still has a beginning, a middle, and an end. But subjectively, it operates outside of time itself. You might experience a kind of living death through these types of voids. You could also feel existential angst with loneliness, but with consciousness it can also include a sense of blessing, of being watched over even while in the bowels of hell. Though no one can save you, sensing the presence of sentient others can make all the difference. My own dream-like version of the void looked and felt like the following.

I'm in a void. I can't quite remember if I'm sure of sentient beings. I've forgotten the light beyond, all those near-death experiences and spirit-beings coming to me in the night. The visions of people I was told I would meet soon and did are growing dim. Now my god has abandoned me, and I am fighting hard not to abandon myself.

Some time ago, when I first felt the void approaching like a storm, I went into my own therapy, hoping it might be my salvation. It worked for a while. But even that time came to an end, and I am now left to further individuate, following an undefined path. I have lost a sense of love and ego-identity. I no longer care about work or friends. It sounds like depression, but it is not. It is an absence of all I've been and all I've known. I can't find myself anywhere. I am now unfulfilled by life and waiting for death, only not ready to go yet. I'd at least like to make some sense of where I've been. I am weary.

In the evening cold, I am carelessly sitting on the frozen ground in my back yard. A cricket at the end of his life hobbles stiffly over to my foot. I gather some grass and lay it beside him. Then I shelter his little body with a leaf. What if life is not necessarily approving but about living with compassion? Loving sunsets, loving seasons, loving hate and—I don't think I can—even violence and death. It's not easy to love grief and pain, ugly words and acid rain, soldiers ripped apart by the new improved M-22. It's not easy either to love my brittle, wounded self. Use "infinite care" with yourself, someone once told me. "Over time, it will teach you to thrive." I vaguely remember wise words Native American author Jamie Sams wrote about this, and of the void itself, but I am moving too close to the void now to hear anything well.

Spending time fighting the inevitable void that is sucking me in, I still do not value the wisdom I might gain from this time as much as I resent the scars it seems to be creating. I want more time to get it right, to be okay, to enjoy living, to feel secure and whole and loved. I don't know why I expect time to provide all these things, although there was a time it did. I can't seem to get back to the garden before that damn snake slithered in; I remember what ease used to feel like but now I find none. Time taunts me and casually waves its long, fruited stems in the summer breeze, just out of reach and oblivious to the grinding of my teeth.

I keep dreaming the same short dream. I am running away from a man and keep running through sand. I never get away, and I never get anywhere. I awake and know that somehow I have to surrender, but to what or whom I don't know. In the depth of my resistance, I don't know if surrender means "fuck it" or "face it," or if it can instead become a kind of harmonic dance between the two. I don't know how to do the dance, but if there is any hope, perhaps I will learn—in time.

And then it just happened. I must have exhausted myself. After spending months fighting the dark world of the void, through depression and existential despair, I finally just stopped resisting. I stopped fighting, complaining, crying, worrying, and trying to manipulate my circumstances. I began to awake each morning saying "This is the day as it is. I am as I am. So be it." My outer world still seemed vague and unreal, as I did to myself, yet I began to rest in the ensuing sense of strange comfort that came over me. Everything felt very simple. I did not write or talk about it. I just did it. I *was* it. The void continued for a few months; then, inexplicably, it was over. A natural rhythm reconnecting me with nature and the passing of the seasons ensued. Being free of the darkness was a rebirth. In time, I was able to return to all I'd loved. My reverence for spiritual beings returned, as did my love of life, friends, work, and of my faithful companion, moose.

I learned to navigate this transition by willingly going into the void. Ever since that time, though I returned to the work and friends I love, I am different. Now I live more often in the mystery, and when I take up my weapons to fight, I put them down rather quickly, knowing that time is not really my adversary. It is only my perception of time that has been my enemy. After years of dis-ease with the limitations of time, I am now accepting my life with more ease exactly as it is.

It is the end of summer now, and this evening I am ensconced in my favorite cabin in the Bitterroot Mountains, far from my own country home. Crickets are chirping here too, just as loud as earlier at the outset of the void I experienced, but rather than a cacophony, now their voices sound sonorous; their song is rich and deep. This time I have trekked far into the sheltering woods, breathing in the cadenced steps of a young moose walking deftly upstream, who only offers a fast backward glance at my smiling face. I have time to watch his disappearing body and the setting sun. The day changes, he changes, I change. It is as it is, and it is good.

22
No Earthly Escape

The only way out is through.
—Johann Wolfgang von Goethe

I have kicked off my dirt-clogged garden shoes and retired to the shade with a cold lemonade. My body aches today. It's been aching for several months now. I never know if it's because I'm often taxing it through exercise or because I'm developing joint problems or hormone deficiencies, or maybe I am just aging. Funny how I toss out the aging part, like it's really nothing, just age, degeneration, and pain. It is one thing to dance on the high wire of psychological passageways; of course such positive affirmation of strengths, wisdom, and maturing character are important. It is another matter to move in a finite human body, wondering why it's getting so hard to get up in the morning and why after sitting for a while my hips are stiff.

My physical energy seems more limited these days, and I don't know if I'll ever recover it. Is it gone for good, like the last goose to fly south for the winter? They return; will I? I don't want the hard things of the world anymore. Weariness pulls at the marrow of my bones, stretching my sore muscles. My mind is tired, too. All I know to do now is rest, hope to recover, and be very, very kind to myself. There is still so much to love and adore here on earth; I do not want to leave a moment before I have to.

But lately it is harder to hike very far to see the moose I love.

Robyn Bridges

I used to think that all challenges were mini-rehearsals for a good death: lessons in how to let go, change, and move into the unknown. These days I think more about how important it is to just love: love who you are, love the passing of a day, find joy in the awareness of how your hand moves, how your mind works, how people can talk and understand, love and interact. These small pleasures are no less miraculous than your first great love, the fragrant iris of summer, or the quiet hush of snow in winter.

A small wire dinosaur from a local florist sits on top of my desk. As I write, he peers down at me. He sprouts little round green leaves and even smaller purple clustered flowers that peek out of his mossy body. His wire head is arched as though saying "Hello!" I have to smile when I see his preposterous being, yet some deep primal remembrance stirs in me, some recognition that his body has indeed given fertile growth to the earth. As I age, I sense that I am a modern dinosaur. In certain ways I am a throwback, preferring to live with less electricity, less modernization, and fewer forms of technology. I avoid shopping malls, overcrowded conditions, and most fads. And though I don't look unusual and actually fit in well in most situations, I tire of other's judgments about my perceptions. Anyone who has felt her own body melt into a moose's and says that moose are her teachers lives outside the norm of modern society. At times I've lived my life in some sort of apology to "realists," but it alternates with anger toward those who can't understand that a person can be reasonable, logical, and intelligent while also being intuitive and alive to a numinous spirituality. Yet when I remember who I really am and the great soulful inner riches I have found on the inner landscape, I am less bothered by those who think me odd.

I do belong on this earth, as the dinosaur did. My people are the stone people, my gatherings the fairy councils. Actually, I know that there are many of us worldwide; some of you are reading this book right now. You are my people, and I am yours.

The strong morning sun has called me to leave my desk and tend to the persistent weeds that flail through my flower garden. I bend, pull, and occasionally curse. Soon my back is aching, and within an hour, my face is sunburned. The wee folk, little fairies and devas who seem to giggle as I perspire, don't have these problems. Knowing this and thinking of them, I stand between two worlds: the realities of earth and the magic of the other worlds that dwell so close to ours. How gifted we are to have human minds that hold this other-world knowledge as well as the emotion to feel it! How lucky we are to have human bodies with which to walk the earth. And how difficult.

My thoughts fade as my physical energy responds to a glass of cold, sweet lemonade. I toss my feelings of separation into the growing compost pile, find another shady spot, and slip off my garden shoes to curl my toes into soft, damp grass. Later, this fall, after the iris have yielded their blooms and the wild strawberries their fruit, I'll spend more time inside and ease my aching bones. I'll have lived today working, and stretching, and clearing space. Tomorrow I think I'll take my old bones up the trail where I saw a momma moose and her baby last spring. I thrill just thinking of it. I will grab my best hiking boots and just go a mile or so in. I can take aspirin or a bubble bath later. Today I am glad to be alive, even in an aging body that aches.

23
The Shaman's Way

Become "Other" as your prayer to the Infinite; there you can effect change.
—North American Shamanic Teacher

Perhaps one of the greatest gifts I've received from my years of placing myself in moose habitat is to allow a direct, shamanic type of encounter with these extraordinary animals. By this I mean that, like the shamans of old who moved into the wise spirit of animals or plants to gather a cure for their patient, I can move into the energy field of "moose" for my own cure.

Today I seek a release from my narrow vision and stuck place. I am despairing such a lonely life with no guarantee of change. Yet whenever I gaze on moose, I simply allow my whole being to empty out and, with a felt sense of his permission, allow my ego self to fade and his presence to consume me. I actually feel myself entering into his body and begin to breathe his breath, be the beating of his heart, look out through his eyes. Though personally almost shocking, visually it is a very subtle process; someone passing by would only see me standing very still and looking mesmerized. And I would be, because for however long I chose to maintain that state (or it chose to allow me to be there), I would forget my self, my ego, my needs, my cares. What a relief. I would become mercifully immersed in another's life, one who has special medicine for me. This is what shape-shifting means at its core: the ability to completely lose one's own sense of physical, mental, and emotional being to enter into another's for sustenance, prayer, understanding, and healing.

When you are willing to have such an experience, you never know quite what you'll experience at the time or what you'll take away from it, but that is part of what makes it so wonderful. With a bit of practice, you will succeed and get what you need, whether a teaching about a needed perceptual change and some sort of life encouragement, a correction, or a new way of being that will help you. For example, at times when I've shape-shifted into a moose, I've realized much more fully how to thrive while living alone. Because I've felt it so viscerally, I remember it for a long time, and the truth of it tends to live in me.

You can experience the essence of all life forms, if you so desire and if it is your medicine to do so. Once I went completely into the spirit of a stone and got in touch with ancient, slow rhythms that helped me to honor and slow my own. Another time I became the ear of an elephant and felt all the large heat-cooling membranes and listening capabilities. I still feel that experience to this day. All that matters is that you allow shape shifting to occur with an open heart and mind, knowing you are safe in the arms of sentience.

Anyone can do this form of shamanic shape shifting if drawn to do so. Skeptics may never allow themselves this experience, yet I still imagine that if at a deeper level they really want to know, they will and be glad for it. You must suspend disbelief, or go ahead and disbelieve but let your desire override it. I must say that my own shape shifting has not happened by my personal will but seems to have come to me at certain times I can't predict or control. A formal shaman can do so at will; my level of encounter is the "I'll show up and just recognize and act on the energy if I feel it there." That has worked for me. I don't like trying to force an experience to happen; I prefer to let it come to me as a part of the "I-Thou" dance of life. However, you may feel fine about using your personal will to achieve such experience. Either way, it is helpful to remember that it may be best to not seek the experience for its own sake; seek to live well, and appropriate experiences will follow. When you do have shape-shifting experiences, you will be the richer for them and may marvel at the profundity of life. "If this is possible," you may say, "what isn't?"

When I shape shift into moose time, moments are strung together by old, learned instinct. When I am in a moose body, I simply notice the way the sun travels across the sky, how the moon passes overhead, and hear the birds who alert my already alert, large ears as to exactly what other animal is nearby, whether it be a lynx, a deer, a wolf. *I do not have human thoughts; I have an ancient knowing. My oblong nostrils catch all scents: I know what is going on in the valley below me and when fire is raging even miles away. I am effortlessly in touch with all my ancestors; all who have preceded me crowd in on my keen senses. I am not separate from them, even though I live alone. I grieve loss directly and fully; then I know when it is time to depart. I do not think like humans do. Though I may return to the place my calf was killed the season before and remember, I know she is gone now, simply gone; I will expand my rib cage with a large sigh and move on. I love to eat mossy fronds but do not miss them when they are not there. I eat what is available. I am steady because of what I know and how well I take care of myself. I have a true confidence rarely seen in humans. They could learn from me.*

This is what it is like to utilize shamanic energy to have a body and mind experience of otherness. I suspect it is what naturalists Walt Whitman, Ralph Waldo Emerson, and John Muir have all alluded to in many of their writings and what inspired some of their environmental stances. It is what indigenous societies are talking about when they say "Talk to Eagle" or "Go on a vision quest." They mean that *you must have an actual, palpable, personal, intimate encounter with the deepest parts of your human self through a felt knowledge of some aspect of nature that wants to gift itself to you.* You willingly surrender your own lonely, longing, hopeful and hopeless places—indeed, every way you would know yourself—in order to fully experience being a part of another life form, be it an animal, plant, or stone person. By experiencing their otherness, you become connected to everything. When you experience another life form, its physical body, mind, heart, and spirit as yours, life is never the same again. Now you know more. And you are forever changed.

Many of you know exactly what I'm talking about and may be far more adept than I at shape shifting. Others of you have experienced something similar to it and may only now be able to put it into context. Yet others of you may not have had any of these kinds of experiences but on some level are getting ready to, or you wouldn't be reading this book. You are the lucky ones. The thrill of first discovery is a lifetime remembrance. For those cynics who find all of this unbelievable, distasteful, or religiously or morally questionable, I say, "Okay, at the end of this life I'll see you on the other side. Sorry you won't get the great thrill of this experience in this lifetime." After all, death is the great shamanic teacher. It is then we truly and finally leave our bodies to merge with the Great All, contributing our consciousness to the vast receptacle of loving presence.

While you're still on earth, however, with a bit of luck and following your own instincts, you can have your own personal shamanic preview right here, right now, in the utter amazement of our beautiful earth. You can live the shaman's path and bring back good medicine for yourself and others. It's as easy as falling in love, and more available. Nothing is withheld. You only have to fall into the long body of your desire and into the willingness of another waiting life.

24

When You Believe

Everything is possible when you believe.
—Kiowa elder

We are lunching at a refurbished railroad station. Two out of the four of us at our table are discussing a friend's recent automobile accident and her resulting paralysis. "There's a reason for everything," the petite, dark-haired woman is saying. One of the two other women nods and smiles. I am more interested in the one who doesn't smile; she catches my eye. She, like me, wants to believe the seeming comfort of this statement and yet is unable to. She and I remain caught between heaven and earth, fate's passengers and heaven's hopefuls. Something keeps me from crossing over to that predetermined land the way I might have when I was young and fresh. Could I let go of such somber hesitation for just a moment?

The women so sure of their beliefs had led fairly safe and good lives, though not without their own share of sorrows. I could not wrap my mind around how they could trust that way. I respected and even envied that they could. Maybe someday I will. Contemporary channeled beings like Seth (Jane Roberts) and Abraham (Esther and Jerry Hicks) claim that we are the complete creators of our experience and that we are solely responsible for attracting all of our own experiences. They also say we can have whatever we want and must simply accept that as we ask, the universe gives. We then must focus on and feel the positive emotions connected to our desires in order for them to manifest. I work with this approach quite a bit and find it helpful, but I still have a few quandaries with the larger questions it presents. I can't quite wrap my mind around it all.

Some great sages follow the idea of events being preordained, but others don't. It is hard to believe that some benevolent force beyond us reasons out everything that happens. That would seem like a parent who has it all planned out, masquerading as one who cares, yet allows horrific suffering and tragedy. During my divorce I left fundamentalist, literal Bible-thumping, hell-and-damnation, Jesus-is-the-only-way Christianity because the doctrines could not satisfy enough of the hard truth of my experiences. What reason could I believe in for suffering, loss, and despair? How could I stop hiding behind a God who did everything for me, including taking responsibility for my life? I considered that the belief of God having a wonderful plan for my life could at times be a shield against my greatest fear that not only am I not in control, but neither is God.

Without a sheltered paradigm, now I have to go more naked into the terrors of life than I did when I believed in "everything for a reason." Life can be hard and heartbreaking. Perhaps my youthful trust began to crumble when I first began to rely on nature as a more reliable antidote than a judging God. Somehow I could move into the Great Mystery in nature; it seemed to infuse even the most scientific or existential explanations. I instinctively knew that the hand of God dwelled there, and that all life forms could support each other—and me. That is when I first met moose, and my life, thank God, has never been the same. I am freer from religious belief yet closer to God. I know less, but I feel more. I have fewer answers but am better able to live the questions.

Animals do not need belief systems to get them through life. They are equipped with natural defenses, instinct, and, if lucky, the habitat in which to thrive. Moose's guard hairs are rounded and full of the best insulation possible; moose change diet in winter to survive and know how to find one another for mating. They have all the basics covered. But who protects them (other than humans, who need to serve as gods and goddesses of habitat preservation)? What god shields them or their young from being mercilessly preyed upon by ravenous wolves? Who protects our own predation?

The two women I'm out to lunch with have cultivated such a seemingly relaxed attitude about life. How can they believe that sorrow, famine, and disease are all part of the "Greater Plan?" How quickly would they say so if they were the subject of such great misfortune? Can their stance lead to greater compassion for the world's ills? I do not find greater lovingness in my own mind when I try it on for size, only a refusal to feel pain. I assume my life would be easier if I could trust in God as the master chess player once again, yet all I know to be my truth is that we originate from the source of all things and will return there. This larger picture is what helps me take responsible action in life. It reminds me that we are all related, regardless of what we believe.

Oddly enough, I have learned about this interrelatedness from the long, brown guard hairs that so perfectly shelter a solitary moose from winter's harsh breath. What grand design to so carefully protect the moose's body temperature! When I have magical encounters with moose, I have allowed my sense of human self to shrink and my sense of animal skin, heart, and mind to increase. This is initially very hard to do, since it means letting go of ego and of how we relate to ourselves and to others in the world. It requires a kind of wild abandon into the heart of nature, where we learn to flow with whatever takes us—a river, a tree, or a moose slipping into the underbrush. We learn to first let go of ourselves in order to get everything back, including ourselves. In altered states I am kin with moose, lost in the reverie of shared time spent with a wild creature who steadily and thoughtfully adds me to his own life experience.

Afterward, the moose I've seen will move off deliberately, deftly crunching through underbrush. The forest will completely camouflage him even as he glances back at me. And I will never be quite the same. Ordinary consciousness returns with a sense that everything will simply turn out as it does amid the teeming, pulsing life around us. This is what I have learned to trust: no matter what our varied opinions, beliefs, or habits are, we are still all connected, and life will be what it is. My addictive nature, which worries and demands that life turn out the way my ego desires, is quieted. A larger force is at work, and I become the dancer and the danced.

When I return to moose country and smell their scent, a quiet, strong energy places itself against my back like an invisible hand. I can recall that welcome pressure even now, far away from the animals I love, and it holds me erect, lifting my ribs and turning my eyes straight ahead. Though I do not seem to be able to believe in godly reasons for everything, I am accompanied by a larger network of support: quiet footfalls, and a tall, brown shape bobbing down a winding path. So it is that I follow; so it is that I live.

Part III

The Medicine of Two-Leggeds

Rejoice in being yourself a beautiful work of nature, and help yourself to further growth; that's the best thing.
—Moses Auerbach

To rejoice in ourselves as a beautiful work of nature can be a difficult task. While we have accomplished great human endeavors through love, compassion, discovery and invention, we have certainly displayed equal or stronger shadow selves: cruelty, betrayal, small-mindedness, and greed. The act of becoming compassionate human beings may be as challenging for us psychologically as it is physically for a moose to keep going after an unbearably long season of drought and a resulting bitter winter. To live well, humans must not only find ways to survive with food, water, clothing, and shelter; as self-reflective beings, we must be able to weather life's harsh conditions while still looking equally upon a bleak or sun-filled morning and say, "This is a good day to be alive."

This final section of *Moose Medicine* traverses the incredibly difficult pathways of learning how to be good human beings. If ever I was pleased with my insights before, now I am primarily humbled. I question. I wonder. I am a learner sitting at the feet of those who have gone before and all who will come, both four-leggeds and two. At the same time, I do claim strengths I have come to realize. Ironically I am able to stand upon certain ground more firmly and am increasingly surefooted in streambeds while learning how to better navigate the bogs of shame and loss.

Therefore, in the spirit of redemption, the chapters that follow attempt, like a benign but purposeful moose, to trot us from shame and abandonment to freedom and belonging. They nudge us away from withholding love from others or ourselves and steer us toward giving and receiving acceptance.

I hope that as you read you will join up with your own dreams and results of what it means to you to be a good human being. I'll be seeing you along the path, maybe in one of my favorite willowed streams, and together we may converse, treading along beside a moose's hoof prints so deftly left in the river sand for us to follow.

25

From Shadow to Light

In my end is my beginning.
—Mary, Queen of Scots

Though moose are experts at the art of camouflage by hiding in trees and shadows, they also know when to come out into the open. Nature is honest: it does not carry deception or guile, but simply the wisdom and utility of whatever the present need. Some of its actions, from the above-ground activity of tree growth to the underground processes of decay and mold, are performed as a visible part of the greater process. Others are performed deep underground, in subterranean waters or in the inner cambium layers of very old trees. We too have underground processes, and when we allow nature to teach us, we may realize that what is hidden can become part of the compost for renewal. In that end is our beginning.

Yet in this new beginning, we stand on the shoulders of the compost that has come before. That compost holds our transformative processes of turning shadow to the light. Because I look to nature for the answer to everything, I wonder why animals do not seem to have shadow natures. They do not feel a compunction to hide who they are or to judge those who do. They simply *are*. What is this difference? Why do humans have shadow tendencies and animals don't? Sometimes to explore our truths, we must navigate questions the way a moose navigates marshes that will suck them in unless they pay attention to where they are placing their feet.

It is early autumn, and I am once again tramping in the mountains of southwest Montana. The air is crisp, and the early morning sun is just barely warming my cold hands. I am disappearing down a trail that I know will lead me to favored moose hangout grounds. And sure enough, there she is. A cow moose sleeks out of the willows just to my left by the arcing stream. Just a moment before, she was camouflaged in the cover and early morning shadows. Nature has seen to her needs so well. But now she is willing to come out into the light, and even willing to be seen by me. She barely glances my way, though her telltale ears continue to flick back and forth in my direction. She has no guile. She is so frank, so there, so basic. My ego chooses to hide certain characteristics in my shadow. She doesn't evidence this at all. What are these differences between this moose and humans?

One apparent difference between humans and animals might be our need for ego and their lack of need for it. In my psychological study and belief, the ego is a crucial structure to the human; as it develops, it helps us know who we are in relation to others. It is the "I-Thou" of Martin Buber's spiritual thesis. Without knowing who we are, we are not stable and functioning; we are psychotic or schizophrenic because we do not have a solid inner understanding of our own selves. The Western concept of self is much more individualized and personalized; the Eastern sense much more connected to the collective. Yet overarching any cultural differences, every individual psyche must have some sense of itself to be intact. Do animals have a modified type of ego structure? If so, why do they need it? Did they used to have egos that they have now transcended? There I go again, assuming they are superior to us and that we are trying to catch up to them.

Maybe that is exactly where I have formed erroneous assumptions about nature. From my own human wounding, I must have come to the conclusion that I should *not* be human because we can be so shaming; I should be more animal. If I can get back to my animal nature, maybe I can lose my shame that was humanly inflicted on me. Maybe I can lose my ego and not have the ongoing memory of childhood pain defining who I am.

What if I could live more often in the present effortlessly, experiencing pain and loss as short-term events, not as defining life characteristics? Even to this day, when life doesn't go my way, I sometimes feel castigated, shut out, and I retreat into my own shadow, alternately hiding or flaunting insecurity and inadequacy. When I experience physical pain, I am sure I'm being punished (for what, I never know) and become angry with God. When abused as a child, I felt anger at the parent who inflicted it, but could not express it directly, so as I grew, that anger turned toward the Big Parent in the Sky and, in my helplessness, toward myself.

Over time, through the drive to live well (is that built into our DNA?), I have learned from wise human teachers how to approach my shadow parts. They have taught me the importance of bringing my shadow feelings, identifications, thoughts, and actions into consciousness so I can examine them thoroughly. In the light, my compassionate self (which I also learned from these same loving teachers) can bring comfort to the wounded parts that otherwise hide from me. In the light, I am challenged to hold every feeling, thought, and action as understandable, forgivable, and redeemable. If I use my talents and fail, yet allow myself to experience that inadequate feeling in the light, that feeling doesn't have a chance to fester. It just is what it is, a disappointment; keeping it attentively in the light allows it to stay warm and nourished. May I have the courage to stay open in my wounding and let the light heal my experience of pain.

I am still watching the cow moose as the autumn day warms into late morning while I explore the psyche of my inner landscape. When I am overwhelmed with an either too-repressed shadow quality or it has burst out unexpectedly and I am embarrassed, I still heal best by simply walking into nature, allowing the natural rhythms I find there to reassure me. I always feel acceptable while walking up dusty trails, watching deer disappear over the ridge, or finding moose prints in the sand by a streambed. Why is this? What is it that nature offers that soothes me so deeply? And if I ever really discovered why, would that change the nature of the magic I experience? As an adult, have I learned to lean hard into nature because of being single for so long? If I had a strong intimate relationship, would I need nature less? Remembering that even safe, loving human partners can't always support each other completely, however, and shouldn't be expected to do so, I continue to return to nature for renewal. And there, any neurotic or unacceptable parts of me feel wordlessly accepted.

Animals in the wild do not hide who they are. The moose does not apologize for striking out when she perceives danger; the buffalo herd isn't sorry about stampeding. Unlike animals, humans scheme and transgress moral codes, then regret their actions later. Why do we do that? Is it because the very need to set moral codes speaks to the presence of a darker side, an opposite that will hide in our personal or collective shadow until it is uncovered? Is it our task as spiritual sages to offer and accept these shadows and unite the opposites within so we can truly live in peace? The irony in nature is that animals seem to have perfected better ways of negotiating their own wild natures while repressing less. How is it that they can do this better than we do? Is it that they are more evolved or that we are more complex?

Every human can hide a whole range of opposites. We choose certain proclivities, consciously or unconsciously. In the light may be our loving nature; if we deny its opposite, hate will reside in our shadow, surprising everyone when it surfaces. When we accept these opposites within, we often find a great relief; at a deep level, we really knew all along that we contained the qualities we were denying. The mask we have been desperately trying to keep in place can gently expand and transform to include opposites while actually allowing us more loving choices. As we humbly recognize our wide range of emotions and reactions, we open our hearts and minds to others more easily, seeing them as "other selves," or as East Indians say, "namaste" ("Hello, another Myself"). We naturally judge less and accept more, within and without.

My own family has given me opportunity to experience both judgment and acceptance. Though they expressed fierce criticism of me every time I made choices that differed from their values, I often still felt loved (they always provided food, shelter, cultural experiences, travel, and constancy, and my father always seemed to basically approve of me). Yet the sting of their criticism forced me to look at my own shadow. My work was to realize over time that at least some of their complaints did have a glimmer of truth in them. I needed to accept my part and become accountable in areas where I was not behaving responsibly. That became my task: to find the grain of truth, forgive myself, and then blow the chaff (their projections of thoughts or actions they couldn't accept in themselves) away.

Their worst criticisms of me seemed to originate from their feeling I was rejecting them either directly or by my life choices, which was never my intent. I was shocked that because of my difficult but necessary divorce, my family and all my many friends in turn divorced me from their lives. At that point I certainly did not feel loved by them. As a result, I endured a period of no friendships at all, which was a new and lonely experience. Yet in time, I found relationships with new people whose primary task was not to critique me every moment. What a relief! I continued to find loving others who saw my flaws but just smiled, who mostly prompted me to lighten up on myself and just enjoy life rather than trying to live up to some degree of excellence every moment. As I began to bring my own shame to light, I also realized that my own shadow was not only comprised of my shortcomings; I had also housed there the valid ego needs of talent, confidence, and strength, intact but shy to the light of day. I started accessing those qualities and trotting them out more often. Once we're adults, we are really the only ones holding ourselves back.

The bad stuff is history. The opportunity is *now*.

While the cow moose ambles slowly around the stream, she feeds, stops to chew, and gazes around her. As she does, she seems to offer me a greater sense of peace about my differences from her. I can still receive her medicine for my own human condition, even though we are not a species family. As I bring the shadow of shame and inadequacy to light, the love available to me on the very air I breathe becomes astounding.

My ego shrinks and becomes less identified with whether I'm wounded or even healed. I simply open, in an act of faith prompted by urgency, to the perception of love by noticing the way a bird flies, the way the cow moose meets my gaze, the way kindness lilts in the breeze. I allow all these pleasant feelings as I stretch my body and appreciate consciousness itself in the moment. This depth of accessible love takes my breath away; it is the same love I feel whenever I walk up a mountain stream or dangle my feet over an old wooden bridge, remembering the moose that has just ambled by. I can't tell you why being in nature always feels loving. Is the gift of nature to allow us to be renewed as well as learn helpful ways of emulating it?

Could we truly begin to awaken to a faith that sees and feels ourselves a part of the natural order of things, rather than hold our human natures separate as antithetical to the wisdom of nature? "Faith," claims author John O'Donahue, "is the helpless attraction to the divine." Seeing a creator's hand in nature is not difficult. O'Donahue continues, "If you look at God as an artist, then it totally alters what you think of God." Could we even see ourselves, shadow and all, as part of the handiwork of God, not some unfortunate mistake? Could the shadow be waiting to be redeemed by realizing our error in having shamed ourselves? I believe that is what has happened for me in my own healing realizations.

As we become more natural in our comfort and familiarity with the process of shadow work, we dip more easily into the darker realms and allow our shadow to see the light of day. In accepting our flaws and learning which ones to transform and which ones to simply let "be," psyche rests.

We become more instinctual and in tune with our own natures. In time we begin to cultivate the Zen-like understanding of the seeming koan, "The dark, the light—no difference." May part of my being a good animal today include my acceptance of my all-too-human tendency to hide qualities and actions in the shadows and to know when to bring them to light. May my need for a valid ego satisfaction stay instinctual and unadorned. And may I stride with confidence around each new bend of life streaming through me.

26

From Abandonment to Belonging

It doesn't interest me if there is one God or many gods. I want to know if you belong or feel abandoned.
—David Whyte

Do you belong or feel abandoned? When do you feel most or least connected? I am most lonely when I do not feel I belong to other people or places, when I am not at home in my body, and when I cannot find a whisper of God, even through nature. In these moments, I move into an existential angst. This dis-ease is only relieved through an eventual return to belonging, through opening to loving and being loved by others, places, and nature. I activate these attentions to free myself from isolating or depressing perceptions and resulting actions that would move me away from the heart of belonging both to myself and to others.

Artists and writers give us eloquent pictures of the contrast between belonging and abandonment. In David Whyte's compelling book of poetry, *The House of Belonging,* he details the many aspects of our human need to be affiliated. Another who writes beautifully about belonging is Irish priest John O'Donahue. In his book *Anam Cara,* he writes, "nowhere do we feel so fully encountered as in the presence of another human being," although I must say that I have felt every bit as much encountered by animals in the wild as by other humans. To belong is perhaps the most primal of comforts. Yet at some time in our lives, we all face the despair of loneliness. We are so afraid of being starkly alone and the resulting feeling of abandonment, which may be the most severe of all dilemmas.

In nature we also find the despair of abandonment. Some time ago I visited a baby moose who had been brought to a recovery center near my home. Actually, he had only been left to nap alone, as is the habit of moose mothers; like a fawn, the baby stays hidden while mother forages, and she returns at regular intervals to nurse. Local residents, who should have known better, misunderstood this and, finding a baby alone, assumed it had been abandoned. They took the calf home, tried to feed it for a few days, and then called the recovery center director, who, groaning at their ignorance, came and retrieved it. Because of the human scent on the baby, the mother would never accept it back again. Abandonment had begun.

The center's major concern was that the clearly frightened calf might not bond to humans and not allow himself to be bottle-fed, which he badly needed. I visited the young moose's new home, where the center director took one look at my pained expression and offered me a newly warmed bottle to feed him. I entered the young moose's straw-bed stall slowly, watching the baby's eager eyes and ears scan me. I kneeled down slowly, holding the bottle to the height where his mother's teats would be. Smelling the milk, he soon tottered over to me, tentatively stretching his little neck toward his desire. Soon, while still watching me carefully, he wrapped his long lips around the nipple. Then the suckling began in earnest. Though voracious in his appetite, he looked lost and confused. I was moved by his dilemma and wished I could have donated more money than I did to help feed him in the coming days. I didn't keep in touch with the center; I couldn't bear to hear if the moose calf died.

During my own days of feeling abandoned, I imagined a story about him: he bonded to his feeders somewhat, but only for three months. Then he contracted pneumonia and died. His death would be considered a "failure to thrive" from the stress of abandonment. I wept for him, and sang and prayed, feeling the anguish of his abandonment deep in my own soul. I later heard that actually he lived well for six years but then died of an undiagnosed intestinal complication. His life was lived somewhere between my litany of early death and a long, healthy life. I do not know if he felt ongoing despair as he grew, though I imagine he did, so removed from his natural, instinctual environment and the lack of mothering from his own species. How, for example, would any of us feel being brought up by wild animals? Though we might not know consciously what we were missing from our own species, if we re-entered human society, surely our struggle would be great. We need to belong in ways we have ancestrally known.

Intact societies routinely renew their sense of belonging through ritual, which often includes some form of a reaffirming ceremony. In his book *Ritual: Power, Healing, and Community,* Malidoma Somé warns, "Western technology is being put in the hands of people who have lost touch with the spiritual." His book is a plea for the restoration of ancient ritual for treating our modern difficulties. When we recognize our belonging, which ritual helps us to do, we are no longer abandoned. We connect our belonging with valuing the good of the community. Members take a balanced pride in how their individual contributions assist the whole. Children and elders alike are cared for and watched over by both blood and non-blood relations. No one goes unnoticed. No one disappears. In the United States, where achievement dwarfs being and separatism swells as an undiagnosed disease, we have a great deal to heal, both personally and communally.

We who have left our cultural homeland generations ago may tend to wander. We travel, move, and seek to belong, to feel at home. And some of us manage it. Some don't. Some never quite feel at home, wandering either externally or internally for years at a time. We don't have to see only the problematic aspects of mobility; we can appreciate the opposite by reclaiming a goodness of the tradition of wandering. John O'Donahue reminds us that our belonging is temporary and is not meant to become fixated on any one way of being, either through our physical home locations or interior attitudes. We are asked to remember that as we listen to the voice of our longings, we will be called to continually discover new ways of belonging. Perhaps because of my own Celtic (Nordic) ancestry, I find this thought tremendously insightful and true to my own experience. As I've grown and changed over time, I've realized that old ways of belonging become stagnant and outworn and I need to find new ways to inspire my evolving soul.

This awareness has supported me as the winds of change beckoned me to set my sails toward new inner and outer territory. The sense of needing to surrender a former way of being to make room for a new one can strike fear into the heart of the bravest soul. We can dig our heels in and attempt to refuse change. Yet nature teaches us that all things end and cycle around again, the same structures in new forms. We belong, even in our deaths, to this eternal cycle. When we realize this, we can begin to relax and allow change with more ease. John Muir knew something about the tendency of humans to assume that negative aspects of nature were somehow separate from God, yet he seemed to have reached a delicate peace, from being frozen, blistered, and famished when caught in a storm (the death cycle) to the welcomed relief of lower elevations, songbirds singing, and sun warming his body (new life once again). He adjusted to change from harsh to benevolent with deep appreciation.

Sometimes change can rock us to our core. When I was in my late twenties, I had an ultimate experience of a literal life-death-life cycle. It began with a drug-like hallucinatory experience at the outset of what I later learned was a "Near-Death Experience" (NDE). I was in a dentist's chair, of all places, only later learning that I had not been given enough oxygen in the nitrous-oxide mixture. Without enough oxygen, I began to feel all muscular capability leaving me. Too suddenly weak to pull the mask off my face or even to open my eyes to signal distress, I slipped into a vague unconsciousness. For a few moments, I felt utterly alone, helpless, and abandoned. I was in the middle of a visceral experience of a type of void. After initially fighting the lack of control, however, I finally yielded, letting myself go with whatever was to follow. The sense of abandonment quickly left as I began to feel a divine peace and purposefulness in what was happening. Soon I left my body and traveled up to a corner of the room, from where I watched the dentist and his assistant, who had no idea that I was dying, as they blithely worked away on my teeth. Through the eyes of my spirit, I then left the room through the top corner and traveled quickly through a long, dark tunnel. Out the other side I entered into a bright place full of light.

Everything there was as I always felt true home and the divine to be. I heard amazing symphonic sounds never heard on earth and saw colors normally unrecognizable to the human eye. I was still me, but not limited and without ego. I didn't mind not having a physical body. I was in a state of total wellbeing while joining many other spiritual beings. Like them, I realized the wisdom of the ages and immediately knew a universal perspective of love weaving the meanings and experiences of human life. I totally and completely belonged. I was home, beyond my dearest imaginings.

I returned from my NDE, of course, and though over time I have realized the gift of the experience, I still never wanted to return to that dentist again. The only hard part was that initially, when I realized I was dying, I could not surrender into it. When I finally did let go, the rest was easy. My NDE left me with a profound gratefulness because it filled me with confidence and inspiration that our spiritual yearnings have a trustworthy basis.

A sense of the divine seems to be crucial to our sense of belonging. If we bypass spirituality in times of trouble or grief, we may try to ignore feelings of abandonment through distractions and addictions. I know that I have an addictive personality; I am often tempted to dull difficult issues through substances or commonplace distractions rather than sit with whatever emotion is rolling through me. The Zen notion of sitting in mindfulness to gain a more objective observer's point of view actually points me closer to the big picture of life. It gives me the possibility of choosing freedom rather than slavery and the ability to see my addictions as a result of my lack of acceptance of whatever I'm fighting. When I fight what is, I decide, "This is too hard," so of course I seek to comfort that perception. However, since I can't change what is, as long as I resist it, I will need to soothe it. Though I now realize I'll probably spend the rest of my life needing to sit with whatever troubles me, let it speak, and then make conscious healthy choices, I have learned that emotions do move through us; nothing lasts forever. Knowing this saddens me over the inevitable ending of happy experiences yet relieves me during experiences I am glad to see depart. I keep learning what the life-death-life cycle metaphor offers. Each time I complete a cycle, I am better able to accept joy and sorrow with greater equanimity, learning I actually belong to both.

I have seen animals carry their wounding with grace: the bull moose scarred in battle, the cow moose licking the dead body of her stillborn baby, the eagle flying with one damaged wing. Animals seem to accept their situation more quickly than we do; they seem programmed to thrive. We can thrive, too. To ponder nature with a listening ear and open heart helps us restore a sense of our own rhythms and the pulse we share with the trees and their leaves, the streams and their marshes, the moose and their young. When we begin to recognize the ways we belong naturally to the earth, to the seasons, and to each other, we find our part of the great "I AM." We come home to the hearth of our own belonging.

There is a rhythm to nature that responds to our own knowing. When we allow our senses to be moved by the flowing tides, the waves lapping on the shore, and the energetic sunrise and calming sunset, we come into rhythm with the diurnal sun and moon influences. We find a subtle magic as we connect to elemental nature. This I know. This I can be sure of. And being sure of something goes a long way to support me in the great unknown.

When we live in communion with ourselves, each other, and the natural world, our lives become a testament to knowing our rightful place. In harmony with seasons of change, we move from abandonment to belonging, having learned that we will visit each again and again. Through the experience of learning how to better accompany ourselves, we better intuit when it is time to come out of isolation and connect with others once again. Like moose, we can learn to live with a greater grace and a more sure cadenced step. Then we will have come home to ourselves.

27

From Shame to Consciousness

You cannot overcome the enemy until you've healed in yourself that which you find despicable in them.
—The I Ching

"Shame on you."

"You should be ashamed of yourself."

"Have you no shame?"

I so want to banish the word *shame* from the dictionary of our psyches. It seems that we have never benefited from this cruel and unredeemable monster that drips slime over our innocence. My mind has trouble wrapping itself around the whole concept of shame; my spirit flies out of my body when I feel shame coming into it. As I see the damage it has caused in me as well as the hundreds of clients I've worked with, I often ponder where shame actually originated. How necessary is it to our human (or animal) condition? How much does shame develop as a result of wounding from our own unhealed selves?

In addition to being shamed, most of us have also shamed others, usually because we've been taught how to do so. Shaming harbors a long hidden legacy. If our parents and theirs before them were shamed in turn, they probably shamed their own children. In the late twentieth and into the twenty-first century, however, through books and workshops, psychologist John Bradshaw may have uncovered our experience of shame more than any other therapist, providing remedies to "heal the shame that binds us." Once a seldom-discussed subject, the shame is now coming out of the closet.

Shame encompasses a deep internal sense of being hopelessly wrong, disgusting, and unforgivable, and we hide it in the shadows because, of course, we are ashamed of our inadequacies. We have been taught that our flaws and poor choices are beyond bad—they are unredeemable. While religions such as Christianity provide a Redeemer who forgives, the church itself still blasts us with constant reminders of our basically shameful, sinful nature. Some traditional Buddhist teachers will hit students, attempting to awaken them, which can look and feel like shaming, even though the intent may be pure. Most religion and cultures reinforce this sense of the impossible human who requires some form of redemption. We are everywhere beset by our seemingly hopeless shame even about our shame.

As always, I tend to look to nature for answers, feeling that a trustable God created it. In nature, the animal kingdom seems to operate with very few instances of shaming, or at least, few evidences of unredeemable shame. I have never felt deliberately shamed by an animal the way I have by humans, though I have been strongly warned by a cow moose, woofing and pinning her ears, and I've also had my path corrected through a false charge. In nature I have only felt a cautionary rebuke, not personal vindictiveness. My mother would often praise me for an accomplishment in a somewhat strained voice—"Oh, good job, congratulations"—leave the room, and a few moments later return and rebuke me, snarling, "Oh don't you just think you're something." Too young to understand that her cruelty was the projection of her own dissatisfaction with her unlived life and that my successes were too hard for her to bear, I took it on as being my fault. I felt shamed, deeply and thoroughly, yet confused at the same time, not understanding what I had done that was so wrong. The messages were mixed, and it took me years of building confidence in community with healthier others as well as the constancy of nature to begin to trust myself.

Rather than once again romanticize nature and vilify humans, I must admit it's true that some animal species on the surface seem to show us shame at work. If a wolf low in rank dares to steal meat from an alpha wolf, it will be mercilessly rebuked. The resulting cowering and whimpering can look like embarrassment or shame to us. When a wolf is rejected from its pack, it slinks away, tail between its legs, in what we would call a most dejected manner. But is the wolf feeling shame? What if its submissive behavior is just that, with no underbelly of shame feeding it? A lone wolf cannot survive long in the wild; it must find another pack or perish. The correction serves a purpose, and when the reprimanded animal accepts his punishment and changes his behavior, he is usually once again allowed to re-enter the pack. A clear message has been delivered, and peace can be restored.

If only it were so in all our human interactions! I am not alone in my experience of being shamed. I have probably shamed others in ways I don't even see to this day. How often we shame others and continue to punish them in some way. We find them wrong and fundamentally unredeemable. Like an alpha wolf, I can kick others out of my pack with a coolness that startles me. The only redemptive part is that I seldom hold angst against them; they are simply behaving in a way that is continually not working for me, so I release them. Is this wrong? Am I too hard on others? Do I expect too much? When I allow myself a sense of my own human belonging to my humanness, I breathe deep and relax. When I remember that I am truly okay just as I am, I can accept others in their own imperfections. We have so many capabilities. May we focus on those capacities and build upon them to our own betterment. May we all see and feel our own redemption from a loving source, in self, other, nature, and the divine.

In the wild, animals seem to learn from each other and don't shame. Because they have been so clear in their initial expressions of boundaries—for example, by moose indicating "No, you can't browse there," or "Not with my female!"—order is established, at least until the next challenge arises. Forgiveness seems unnecessary for them; they learn whom to approach and whom not to, what is acceptable and what is not, by show of force and dominance. As humans, we think we are more civilized than animals when we seek change through compromise, making decisions based on moral values rather than on sheer force. But how far have we progressed if we still practice shaming without redemption, or even need to shame at all?

One of my clients taught me beautifully about what it is to feel, claim, experience, and move through shame. She was very talented, focused, and driven in her career, and was eager to clear any blockages that would keep her from self-actualizing. When she was aware of the subtle ways that shame was rising in her, especially through perfectionism, she'd identify the context, feel it in her body, make sounds, draw, move, and voice it, and then claim her rightful place instead of the shame. This bringing awareness to the surface allowed an alchemy to ignite. By naming the shame, she unseated its formerly unconscious power in her ego and claimed her preferred power of being capable. The dross turned to gold. I was in awe. It takes a strong ego to do this; you must be confident enough of your basic strengths to consciously allow shame, with its debilitating ways, to become truly conscious. She would always come through the process with more confidence of who she really was; shame was the Great Pretender (though it had a real hold). She cyclically moved from shame to consciousness.

When I feel shame, I now ask my soul what it wants to experience and feel the depth of that desire in my body. The shame might be telling me I am not good enough. So I express that "not good enough" through movement, sound, art, or self-talk. I may roll up in a tight, squirming, fetal position. While doing so, I breathe often and deeply. I might make wrenching sounds that surprise me, but I keep pressing myself to fully express. I might draw black, ugly shapes with big red lines crossing through. During this time, I keep connecting with my spirit, doing my best to relinquish ego needs and asking to be placed in alignment with my higher purpose. Then I might let this shame say every raw and awful thing it thinks so I can root out the blackened, charred roots of unhealthy beliefs and nourish the growth of a healthy fecundity within. The words may sting: unworthy, horrid, undeserving, a mistake. I breathe again. Though I want to recoil, I don't. I let these awful feelings stay lifted up to the light of my consciousness so I can do what comes naturally: love and treat them with compassion. I treat myself as a treasured child who has misunderstood something fundamental about her true self. Then I might find a mantra to hone my preferred awareness, like, "I am completely safe, loved, and accepted by all things in the universe." I repeat this many times until I am at peace once again and knowing my rightful place in the world. All of these actions deepen my sense of self in relationship to whatever shame has become activated in me.

I am remembering now the last time I breathed really deeply without shame or guile. It was late summer, and the sun was beginning to set over the Bitterroot Mountains. While meandering through a willowed thicket, I had just found moose hoof prints in the sand near my favorite pond by the river. I picked up a handful of the sand containing the imprint of the hooves I loved and, giggling with delight, sprinkled it into the medicine bag I was carrying. I was totally a part of the wonder of the moment and not shaming or ashamed of anything there. Let me live in that place, in a connected stream of consciousness, no matter where I wander.

28

The Art of Loving and Letting Go

The lovers visible, and the Beloved invisible—whoever saw such a love in all the world?
—Rumi

The esteemed poet Rumi clearly knew the art of love, both visible and invisible. We can all have this experience of finding love in the human world we see as well as the worlds beyond that we sense. Yet to truly love other humans seems to require a clearing of all the defenses we've built up to protect ourselves. Over time, life can deal a harsh hand; how we respond determines the level of vulnerability we retain. The ability to love and let go through inevitable loss is daunting. How did Rumi accomplish this? He must have learned how to do so throughout his life, as is evident in his writings. Losing his soul friend and love Shaz was devastating, yet he returned to an ecstatic love of God and life. He knew about love.

It seems odd to me that humans seem to need to learn how to love and that true loving is indeed an art. Learning self-love may be the most difficult challenge we face. Might all discord and strife spawn from our lack of this essential skill? Even if we've been brought up in a loving environment, it still has not been a perfect one, because we as a species are not yet perfected. We all need to grow into a greater self-love. Or, if we have not been taught love by example, especially during childhood, then our adult journey beckons us to learn how to love ourselves and in turn love others. If we can do so, we may be like caterpillars fulfilling our destinies; after the cocooning of the "going-within time," we emerge and metamorphose into creatures of beauty. Like the mountains and the wild places of the earth, we become more open and expansive. Like the rivers winding their way to the sea, we find our natural depository of loving expression.

The path of human-to-human love is arduous. After the "in love" of Western romanticism fades, the real opportunity to love arises. It is then we begin to pinpoint unredeemable faults in our partners because we cannot accept our own. Animals do not deal with this, perhaps because they are always who they are. Is it because they have no ego need, therefore no capacity to judge some qualities as more or less desirable, and therefore no need to enhance or hide anything? Will we, too, not have to hide anything when we can accept the opposites of love and hate within ourselves? Have animals already crossed this threshold to live on the other side of transcended opposites?

Animals seem to love without effort. They do not seem to need to learn self-love in order to love others; I think that they simply love by being who they are. Of course they have their own personalities—some are more gregarious than others and some more irritable—but they do not normally express a withholding of general wellbeing. In my favorite mountains in southwest Montana, I watch the way moose take each other in—territorial, yes, but somehow open to the presence of another. I do not know when a cow moose snorts at another cow moose if she is saying, "Don't come near *my* baby," or simply, "I see you there. Here I am." Either way has no guile, just clear boundaries.

That cow moose is not necessarily being loving. Is she just simply being?

Is being itself an act of love in the largest sense?

She snorts and then returns to her grazing. She has no need of these questions or their answers. As I watch her and the other cow disappearing at the far end of the meadow, I have no feelings myself of love or lack of love. Simply being. Again I wonder: Is this its own form of love? Can I lose my own wonderings in the act of wandering in nature, down the paths so surely made by a moose carefully carving out her way, living naturally in her environment?

But I am not ready to just follow her path yet. I keep feeling that to understand more deeply will lead us to greater peace. I follow the track of my own human footprints and the heartbeat of my spirit. I have seldom considered that it is a privilege to struggle with human thought as a path to growth and evolution; I long for ease and a natural cadence without such effort. How is it that animals might not need to learn self-love, but we say that humans need to? Is it true that we need to love ourselves before we can truly love others? Though a cow moose stands quietly beside her dying calf and cannot help with lifesaving measures as we could, does she love any less? Does she love that calf as much as we love our own children? How could we ever know for sure, especially if we are applying our values to her actions? Do we anthropomorphize because we are too lonely and lost as a species? Or simply because we intuit that all things are ultimately connected? Because we don't see her tears or hear her groans, does that prove she cares any less? What if her grief was less intense, allowing her to move on more quickly to recover the safety of her own life? Does this mean she loves herself, even if unconsciously? Is her life the Creator loving Itself?

For humans, love always encompasses forgiveness. Love actually grows through releasing others from our fields of criticism, blame, neglect, or abuse. To forgive is to return to our divine origins. To forgive is to rejoin both ourselves and society, though it does not mean we are to pretend that unacceptable acts were never committed, and it does not keep us from making new boundaries for self-protection. As poet Maya Angelou said of her seven years of silence after being raped: "Forgiveness is not forgetting; it is holding the trespassers accountable for their actions while forgiving the persons involved." If only we would all apply such a wise statement. I am not sure whether I've completely forgiven a few people in my own life. I do not hold out energy against them, but I am not interested in having them in my life anymore and would most likely not accept overtures from them to reconvene. Can I live with myself in peace if I keep them away? Can I come to closure over those events and memories? Can I love and forgive myself for my own ongoing shortcomings?

Many stories have surfaced from the terrors of war, but few have included the aftermath of forgiveness expressed by the following. This account, told at a workshop gathering I attended in California, centers around a soldier from the Vietnam war who had maimed the face of a young Vietnamese girl while following orders from his superior to wipe out a village. Years later, the girl found him and excitedly told him how wonderfully her life had turned out. As he looked at her scarred and still-misshapen face, he broke down sobbing, asking if she could ever forgive him.

"Oh," she smiled, "I forgave you a long time ago. I wanted to see if *you* were all right."

It is never too late for us to embark upon the journey of discovering what self-love looks and feels like. One of the greatest trials of love is through loss and the resulting grief. Moose have taught me a great deal about accepting loss through feeling accepted in their company. Their steady concurrence with life and their ability to adapt to their environment have convinced me that I can do this too, even if it takes a lifetime of practice.

Not long ago, once again deep in the backwoods, I watched a mother moose nuzzle and finally walk away from her dead baby after staying with it for hours. I had come upon them suddenly, startled to see her leaning over her three-month old calf, who was almost completely hidden in the willows in a damp, sandy lump near the river's edge. I couldn't tell how the calf had died, only that it was wrapped around itself in a pile of legs and ears and body. The mother, who had an odd tuft of hair curling over her withers, was breathing rather fast, swaying back and forth, her eyes locked on her baby. I could hardly stay to watch. She saw me but barely cared that I was nearby. I sang a song of blessing for both of them and left. I felt my own sorrow from miscarriages too deeply and just couldn't stay near them any longer. But after hiking for half a day over the next ridge, I gathered myself and decided not to abandon this scene or myself. So I turned around and returned to sit with the sorrow and see it through. As I returned, I saw that she was still standing beside her lifeless offspring. I sighed deeply, her pain and my own blending. But now I began to notice that she was leaning outwards slightly, looking downstream as though something was calling to her—maybe another moose, a coyote, or even a wolf. Maybe she was just realizing that she would need to browse and nourish herself again soon.

As I sat curled up nearby, she stepped back from the baby and craned her neck frankly toward me. I imagine we shared a moment of pure grief. I too knew what it was like to lose little ones, to have dreams turn to damp piles of death. She gazed at me for a long moment, and time ceased, even my breathing. Then she heaved a big sigh and moved off, only flicking her ears once or twice without looking back. I stayed there on the sandy shore crying for a long time after she had gone.

She knew something about acceptance it has taken me years to learn. She knew how to feel love and grief, to experience loss, and then to move on. For any of us caught by grief's fierce embrace, learning to accept loss eventually creates an environment downstream in which we can forage for ourselves once again. We learn to love our lives, ourselves, and each other; grieve; and finally let go because we have truly loved. As we build self-love through forgiveness and acceptance, our cooperation with life increases. As we pair with life, life pairs with us. The art of loving and the art of living become one.

I saw the same cow moose with the curled tufts of hair the next spring only a few hundred yards downstream from where her calf had died. She had a new baby and was engrossed in its shelter and care. The baby looked at me, blinking slowly, and I realized, *This young one knows nothing of me, of the grief her mother and I shared.* And I smiled. I accepted that this new life was good and loved. It was here now, and I was glad.

29

Intimate Broken Places

The world breaks everyone and afterward many are strong at the broken places.
—Ernest Hemingway

It is early autumn in the Bitterroot Mountains. The serviceberries are shriveling with the cold nights, their leaves turning shades of mottled, ruddy red and brown. Aspen are waving their brilliant golden leaves at the air for anyone in the vicinity to notice. I am warmly dressed in my favorite forest-green down parka, just the right color to blend in to the pines. In the sunlit clearing, just yards away from where I am hoping to stay camouflaged behind a massive tree, I am watching a cow moose with her calf. She is grazing on short stalks of wheat grass, and her calf is splay-footed, attempting to do the same. Just then a mangy young moose pokes his head out of the nearby willows. The mother moose barks at him; he lays his ears back, flattens his eyelids, and moves away again.

I saw this same youngster with her last year; I can tell by his short, saucer-shaped muzzle and I know her by her light-brown coat and the sharp angle of her hips. His mother now has a new calf and no time or tolerance for him. Though he tries several times again to approach her, she forbids it. He emits a kind of whine, shakes his head, and disappears back into the willows. Did he feel broken? In that moment, I felt that kind of pain in my own heart.

In that trio, I see both an intact and what seems to be a broken relationship. The cow and her calf evidence trust and vulnerability with each other; we could say they have a "relationship." They certainly show intimacy in terms of how well they know each other. But has the relationship between the cow and her older youngster been broken? It would seem so.

Animals carry what I would call " instinctive bonding." They know when to mate and with whom. They know how to connect with their species, how long to raise their young, and when to release them. Though some species mate for life, and the more intelligent mammals (by our standards) are thought to experience a greater range of emotions, we still do not see the level of emotional or mental complexity that humans evidence. Our species is beset by conflicting thoughts and desires plus a past and the resulting protectiveness and defensiveness that we tend to lug around with us, barring us from the kind of intimate relationships we most long for.

Webster's dictionary defines intimacy as "a private act." Does that preclude animals, in both their inter- and intraspecies relatedness? Do animals share deep emotions? We have no evidence that they are self-reflective, but does that preclude the fact that their instincts might include a type of reflexive intimacy? I have been told by friends who raise herds of buffalo that when one is sent to slaughter, the others grieve. They will stay in the place that their companion was actually slaughtered or trailered away from for days. Elephants have been known to yearly revisit the death site of herd members, and some horses go off their feed when they have lost one of their own with whom they were close.

If animals do indeed experience some form of intimacy, they must also experience brokenness. I've seen a version of it in horse pairings, in one of the many herds of horses I used to oversee. I spent one summer watching a gelding and mare become very close. On any given day, they would be paired up in the pasture, standing head-to-rump, swishing the flies away from each other's faces and gently teething the other's withers. When another gelding joined the herd, however, the mare dropped her old friend and hooked up with the new one. However, the new gelding was soon sold, and when the mare tried to return to her former friend, he would have nothing to do with her. Had trust been broken in a way that ruined their relationship?

My friend and her soon-to-be ex are in a musty courtroom in a county different than theirs. They didn't want too many questions from their own community too soon. "We need time," he said. She had agreed. "Irretrievably broken," the judge pronounced. She said she almost corrected him on the spot. "What an awful statement," she told me later. "This is not broken; this is a hard-won realization, the result of excruciating truths, and the opportunity for new growth and new beginnings for both of us." "Broken" didn't work for me either. During the pronouncement from my own divorce, I felt shards of glass slicing into bare feet I was trying so hard to fit to new shoes. Don't lame me when I'm down and struggling to get up. Help me get up, my community, my culture, my family, to become the best I can be. Don't judge me as "failed," and certainly don't tell me anything is "broken." Our culture embeds our judgments into our language. We revel in judgment about relationships. Look at daytime and evening soap opera television shows. They revel in the pain of the intimacy of the human relatedness dilemma.

What is required for strong, intimate relationship that can thrive through or even because of brokenness? In my counseling work, I have repeatedly seen relationship bonds strengthen when both partners are willing to engage in healing their brokenness within themselves. They begin to help each other heal when each is able to listen deeply and respectfully to the other, sincerely desiring to understand and sometimes adjust behaviors or expectations accordingly. But there's a catch: if one's own wounding or lack of trust is too limiting of his or her capacity to be emotionally vulnerable in the process, the relationship flounders. All healing begins within each person.

What our culture has forgotten is that this form of intimacy is secondary to the intimacy we make and carry within ourselves. If I cannot go to my own depths, how can I accompany others through theirs? How can I share vulnerabilities of trust and compassion if I have not developed them for myself? We continue to seek outside ourselves the things we need from within.

Our individual brokenness is the very crux of our difficulties in relationship. When we project our brokenness outward, where we were wounded, we wound. If we were ignored, we ignore. If we were criticized, we criticize others. If, however, we have instead internalized and therefore introjected our wounding, we correct and blame ourselves for every problem in the relationship. It's all our fault; we are wrong, bad, and unredeemable. The trick is to own our projections and release our introjections. Often, a great deal of therapeutic healing work needs to be done to accomplish this.

Because our young North American culture is adolescent, we don't tend to realize our ability, and indeed necessity, to draw on ancient knowledge for our healing. We don't listen to elder wisdom; we thoughtlessly forge ahead. We don't reflect; we react. We want what we want—now, our way. We have not cultivated the patience to tend to deep relationship. And good relationships take tending.

When humans lack self-approval, self-esteem, and self-knowing, we set up roadblocks to true intimacy. We all do this. We all wound and have been wounded. We take personal offence when none was meant; we criticize and then claim we didn't mean it. The wounds we create and receive never heal when we pick at them. We keep scraping because we are looking to resolve the problem. Yet there is a time to work through the problems and a time to just refocus on love and approval. Then we have to tend to ourselves and "shine the gentle light of soul in to the wound," as John O'Donahue suggests in his book *Anam Cara*. He continues, "When you love someone, it is destructive to keep scraping at the clay of your belonging. There is much to recommend not interfering with your love."

There is, however, a deep personal intimacy offered through struggle. Contemporary author Thomas Moore has written intelligently and thoughtfully about these dark nights. He counsels us to realize that we are not to try to resolve the dark night but rather be enriched by it.

When we allow difficult passageways to break us open, we can then allow the possibility of healing. I have certainly grown stronger from my own broken places, even when grief overtakes me again and again. As I am willing to be present to the truth and depth of my struggles without judging myself, ignoring, or rushing through, I find a deeper relationship within through bravely traversing my inner landscape. The more I discover and then tend to my own needs, the less I expect others to fill them for me. I become less needy in intimate relationships through having mended my own heart and mind.

We are at our strongest when we choose intimacy out of fullness and not out of need. When we can be comfortable alone and know we are complete, we become better partners. The more accepting we have become of our own strengths and weakness, the more understanding we will be of those around us. And the more we understand our individual cycles of romance, intimacy, relationship, and change, the greater our capacity to allow our partners to go through their own changes in their own time. Well-partnered couples or friends allow a cycling of closeness and distance with acceptance and understanding. They trust the cycling and themselves. They also tend to experience more peace and enjoyment than drama and strife, even during times of inevitable conflict. They learn and grow in wisdom and a sober joy.

When intimate conflict does occur, time alone in nature can provide solace for the wounds of a troubled relationship. Because nature is still and has no agenda, it can create an environment where you receive unexpected insight about patterns you want to change and how to do so. In the natural wild, you can experience the earth and its ecosystems as a type of reliable parent and trustworthy other-species friend. When you walk psychologically naked into nature, releasing agendas or self-protective defenses, it can teach confidence, reality, an impartial view, and an effortless sense of belonging. You ascend a mountain or hike a valley trail and simply give yourself over to solitude. Everywhere you see beauty—up that craggy slope, around the corner of this rocky path, in the pungent smell of the juniper you just passed. You can watch birds fly effortlessly from ground to tree, finding the respite of sheltering forests in winter and fresh running water in summer. You can feel your own body rhythms come into harmony with life all around you. Your feet are welcome on the earth, and no one is making you feel bad or wrong about anything. Whatever event comes your way becomes a miracle, a sign, a message. A butterfly alighting near you may offer an answer to a burning question; the way water cascades over a particular rock may be reminding you to go with the flow. Even the breeze can speak to you. What you hear it say always relies on the courage to believe what you intuit. Nature is a great suspender of disbelief. If you want to believe again, you can lose yourself up that mountain trail, beside that rushing stream, beneath that long-armed fir tree. When you decide to spend enough time there, you can remember the reliability of the passage of a day, the rhythm of the seasons, and observe how every aspect of nature is coded for these cyclical changes. When you listen to nature deeply, you can return to your human relatives with a restored heart, able to share the outcome of this sustenance. You can then truly listen to your partner without defensiveness and share your truth with clarity.

Ironically, moving through brokenness together offers great freedom, shelter, comfort, and companionship. The very places that broke become stronger as you come into alignment with the natural rhythms of give and take, personal renewal, and loss. You learn to let a fierce beauty give its gifts and find pathways for your own wild heart to open and give gifts to others who will love and cherish your presence as you do theirs. Your beneficence then also extends to cherished memories of those who have passed on. You strengthen your sense of the ultimate goodness of living and become more connected within yourself, to your partner, to others, and to the natural world. With applied kindness, your intimate broken places can heal. From having absorbed the salve of nature, you are more healed within and carry that strength with you.

30

Reconstructing Conflict

Our deepest fears are like dragons guarding our deepest treasure.

—Rainer Maria Rilke

The crashing suddenly emanating near the west slope of the meadow about half a mile from my cabin sounds strange. It is the end of a clear-blue-sky late-summer day, so it can't be lightning. There are no roads in that direction, so it can't be a bulldozer logging yet another stretch of timbered mountainside. No, this crack and clash sounds more like a resonant echo. I think I can hear something like grunts after each clash. Oh—moose or elk may be in early rut!

I jump off my porch, my book falling off my lap and my tea tipping over. Wearing only a light top, shorts, and tennis shoes in the fading light and evening cool, I race across the meadow as fast as I can to see the excitement first hand. Oblivious to personal danger, I run along, panting, with common sense catching up with me only as I near the deep woods towards the direction of the continued clacking. I slow now, suddenly feeling small and afraid. But drawn by my deep sense of adventure, I have to continue. I weave through a faint game trail, duck under pine branches, and draw closer to the ongoing sounds.

And there they are: two big bull moose in combat. Beyond them, a cow peers out from between several large trees about twenty yards away; she is as close to them as I am. They currently seem oblivious to both of us. The battle is on!

The larger one is winning (in nature, doesn't size always seem to win?). A point of the smaller one's right rack suddenly breaks off, and he does too, grunting and wheeling away, moving off slowly into the south, in the opposite direction of the waiting female. The victor snorts and flaps his ears a few times. Then he glances in my direction; he seems nonplussed about my presence, however, just full of himself. He quickly moves toward the cow, who greets him with an extended muzzle. Exhausted, he drops to the ground, and she joins him. I creep to only ten yards away from them, though mostly hiding behind thick cover. Soon, to my amazement, they are both slumbering.

What could this encounter I've just had teach me about conflict? My feminine self turns away from the patriarchal use of force or size to solve conflict; I am so aware of how peace emanates through the energetic of a gathering in a circle, where all are heard and none are harmed. Though when conflict erupts in nature there can be duels to the death, most stop short of that. The loser realizes he is the lesser and retreats in self-preservation. As humans, if we think ourselves more "advanced," we must find more artful ways of solving conflict, ways not bent around force but sculpted through understanding and compromise.

In the wild, at the close of conflict, the final surrender signal from a mammal will often be to avert his eyes and roll his shoulder away. Perhaps we too may be served by following that model. We might avoid locking horns by using a similar physical stance at the very start of conflict. We could handle an entire session of conflict by sitting shoulder to shoulder, like two sides of a horizontal isosceles triangle, looking at the problem itself as the top of the triangle, out ahead of us. In this way we are avoiding our more primitive animal instincts to square off and butt heads; we have the capacity to choose a "win-win." We focus on the problem and not the persons involved. This act alone can keep tempers from erupting because it allows more emotional distance. We are then essentially shoulder-to-shoulder, working out a problem together. We both focus toward the imaginary third point of the triangle so we can come to a solution together.

You will be amazed how much this helps. It is harder to physically, mentally, or emotionally hurt each other when you stand shoulder-to-shoulder. Your gaze naturally falls to a center point ahead, reminding you that there is an outer issue to be solved. This physical stance helps you focus on the subject at hand, rather than the personality of your adversary, even if it is a personal issue. If we agree to the concept of a "win-win," we should each be able to get much of what we want. We agree that solutions will be acceptable to both sides. This approach helps keep us focused on being problem-solution oriented without blaming the other. It is truly a sophisticated art, and it takes practice.

Every time I'm involved in a conflict where I get upset or my feelings get hurt, or I feel defensive and either say too much or too little, I am humbly reminded of the vast challenge of international peace. I firmly believe that peace begins at home. If I cannot make peace with family, friends, or coworkers, from where is the larger collective of world peace going to arrive? I pray that it is true that we evolve as a species, because with our precarious world situation in the twenty-first century, we desperately need to! That is the unique challenge to our species: to discover how to create peace ourselves. And time spent alone in nature can activate the very heart of peace that we can then bring back into the more complicated world of human thought and emotion.

Diverse points of view can live under one umbrella of unity. Sages have said that we have incarnated on earth to be individual parts of God—I am perhaps a hand and you, a foot. When I see that you have loves, dreams, hopes, and disappointments like I do, I can see more of our commonality and stop treating you like my enemy. And if our two opposing sides have the wisdom to see that both are part of the larger sentient universe, we will better meet our global and personal challenges and keep refining a workable peace. Nothing less will do.

The blue jay ceases her incessant squawking when the hawk decides to move elsewhere, the moose her woofing when the human departs, the two elk their fight when one wins. This seems to be based on power and strength, yet none of those species creates global war.

The urge and call of peace is ancient but never more imminent than today. Might we glean from nature how to set boundaries fairly, to know when to retreat, and to consider that we can link with all animals and plant life to birth ourselves into a new world that has learned how to transcend killing as a way of resolving conflict? We are on the brink of destruction; it only makes sense that we should be putting all our energies toward finding peaceful solutions for all our ills. I am convinced it is possible and that nature can provide the structural support for us to proceed. Then we have to trust the natural ability of our human minds and spirits to show the way. May we link with all that breathes life to find our own natural path to wholeness.

It is late winter now; I step briefly into my back yard in early morning before going to work just to reacquaint myself with quiet moments in the cold and snow. I wander around, crunching through the white plumes, noting fresh deer and rabbit tracks. From the deep snow impressions at the far end of my property, I see that several deer have apparently slept in the "fairy grove," a round clumping of trees with a stone bench in the center. I cannot help but smile. I am so glad to be sharing the neighborhood with them. I see how they get along, find their place, and I seek to cause as little conflict for them as possible. I am following the tracks of their sentience, one step at a time, and, as my Indian friends like to say, *It is good.*

31

Recognizing Your True Purpose

The mind loves to know: Who am I? What am I here for? So let it find out. Release the struggle. Just move toward that which you deeply love, and you will find out.
—Anonymous

As developing and thoughtful humans, we have an inner drive toward meaning and knowing our life's purpose. Often it drives us to existential despair. The fact that most wild animals do not evidence this need intrigues me. How have they escaped the need for meaning? They appear to live simply, seemingly content with or at least aware of who they are. Their acceptance of life's varied conditions is both a model and a frustration. Why is the search for meaning and purpose both so necessary and difficult for humans? Though some say that this opportunity to grow through struggle is our privilege, my naïve and childlike self wonders why we can't just browse through life, operating on instinct, happy to have enough water, food, and sun. But my adult self knows that whatever I might prefer, life is still going to be a challenge.

Most humans seem to experience some degree of spiritual dilemma: does God exist? How do we fit in? What is the role of suffering? What is our purpose? Nature can assist us by providing a safe, contemplative ground in which to decipher deeper truths, but we may find the most specific help through other two-leggeds who carry the wisdom of ancestral discovery. Through them, current human inquiry, and experience with divinity itself, we can find a platform that suits our need to work out our salvation.

As we develop the contours of our inner psychological and spiritual landscape through seeking answers, we grow stronger antennae with which to hear our life's purpose. We begin to craft our values through making meaning of our life experiences. The conclusions we draw about the suffering or well-being we have personally known may influence the way we construct our spirituality and our need for personal purpose. I don't see this self-reflection evident in animals, and one theory is that they have no need of it. I wonder if it isn't more that they evolved through that need themselves and are just waiting for us to do the same. Isn't the highest knowing an effortless oneness with the "All That Is," a non-reflective being-ness evident through fully inhabiting one's life? Yet whether we are still trying to catch up to the advanced sentience of animals or are simply different, the human dilemma remains: How can we live fully with psychological meaning and spiritual satisfaction?

At one point in my own life, while receiving my own healing therapy, a safe and loving therapist told me that when others were sad like I was, they had curled up in her lap while she sang to them and stroked their hair. Though I had already begun my own therapy practice serving others, I parked my ego, let myself truly become the client once again, and curled up with her. Tears of relief came with deep sighs of having safe human harbor. I remembered that I could actively love myself through the inevitable dark passageways of living, and that I too could come out on the other side singing, as she did for me in a healthy and nurturing way. I have carried with me the sense of total peace and acceptance through the simple act of leaning into her earthy embrace.

Time spent in nature has taught me a natural spirituality, yet it doesn't release me from the need to mindfully develop a working spirituality. Every time I consciously allow an integration of my humanity and my spirit, I participate in a practical mysticism. When I am embodied in this way, I show up on time and can organize the practicalities of life, yet also carry an intact sense of the divine in my personal sphere and view of the world at large. This seems so different from what animals seem to do effortlessly. They show up on time to feed, mate, seek lower pastures in winter and higher in summer, and likely evidence many more behaviors of which only professional naturalists or very keen observers are aware.

Why, after all, should nature need to seek the "All That Is," Great Creator, Goddess/God, when it is already the expression of the Divine? Are humans just as expressive of the divine? When we search for spiritual connection, we often actively seek time apart from other humans to connect with the nonhuman world, to glean the magic from animals, plants, the standing people, the stone people, and otherworld inhabitants like angels, ancestors, and other wise beings. I've never known of wild animals seeking to spend time with us, although perhaps that is the next frontier for me to recognize; many of my astute friends already believe that.

I am most content when I have a spiritual cosmology to steer by that promotes a strong sense of being without feeling a relentless need to achieve. However, when I start thinking of myself as separate from God, I can become ego-driven and value "doing" over "being." One day some years ago, I was particularly struggling with my insatiable need to succeed. Was what I accomplished my only value? Was I nothing without success? I was at ease with how my career had evolved over time and with the current therapy I offered to others, but I often felt a rude inner drive to continually experience more success and not to rest until I was done. This urge left me nervous, weary, and depressed. Couldn't I rest? Couldn't I buy a ticket to life by just being? And perhaps most fearful of all: Who was I if I was not at least attempting to accomplish, to do, and to exceed all expectations?

One summer afternoon I was contemplating this internal fight between doing and being on my back porch while gazing over the alfalfa fields all around. The full sun overhead and tree-lined mountains in the background created a sense of deep content. A bald eagle had just flown by when a bluebird alighted on a fencepost close to me. Without thinking, I began lifting my hands in praise of the beauty of the natural world, and suddenly I knew how being and doing could be interconnected. "Ha, ha!"

I laughed aloud with palpable relief. "My purpose is to love and praise the beauty of creation!" I'd been doing my being for years, consciously loving and blessing all of creation daily. Ironically, all that I had accomplished had been springing naturally from that pure source.

Accomplishment in my chosen profession was good but not, I finally realized, a requirement from some demanding god. I finally was able to release myself from the fierce demand of servitude to that god as well as to the closely related inner critic I'd been listening to for years. From that moment on, I began a major healing that still carries energy to me every day by activating my sense of joy without obligation and freedom without self-castigation. As I age, I am much freer of the need to accomplish, but still on occasion have to stop and rebalance my tendency to either work too hard or to become dormant. It is a dynamic choice, a dance of respecting my "work-play" rhythms. When I choose consciousness, I find peace pervading both my being and my doing, both work and play. It is good to live this way.

Your true "doing your being" involves learning to live and act in a grounded manner with honesty, courage, and an eye to the heavens. No matter the degree of your awareness of your life purpose, you are on the path to your purpose already because you are living life. However, if you want to progress in your understanding, you may need to seek conscious living by plumbing the depth of your desire and, as Joseph Campbell popularized, follow your bliss. In her book *The Purpose of Your Life*, Carol Adrienne reminds us to be clear about our intentions. Are you being your true self? The surest way to know that you are fulfilling your purpose is simple, she tells us. Are you feeling joy and a deep commitment to that which you love? Though after the third time reading her book I was still unsure of my purpose, it somehow helped me to finally let go into my life. I learned that you must take time to understand what bliss means to you and how to integrate it into the practical world. You may choose to make a living doing your bliss or not. Even if your work does not feel soulful in itself, you can still bring soulfulness to it by who you are. Are you full of spirit and life? I am not talking about an upbeat, cheerful, or extroverted persona. I am talking about the deep intangibles of a soulful presence cultivated in the caverns of the heart. When you deepen your inner connection, you will naturally convey this fullness.

With my back-porch epiphany, I recognized that I could be free of the wounding that had caused me to not trust myself and that no one was keeping me from doing what I wanted to do. When I began to believe I could both know and actually live my purpose, I was ready to receive. And I did. As a result of learning to be, a natural "doing" developed. Now, through my private practice, workshops, and retreats, I share ways of developing psychological and spiritual astuteness through nature. A struggled beginning has evolved into an effortless, though at times hard-working, accomplishment. For now, and in the foreseeable future, this is my path. And when that changes, may I have the wisdom to do my part and then wait to see how I will be filling the next step of my process of conscious living.

You may have multiple purposes: a personal purpose, a work purpose, a community purpose, and a purpose in relationship to nature, country, place, cause, or another person. Some purposes may morph over time. Though being of service to others may be demanding, if you feel in your bones that it is at least your temporary purpose, you will perform with ease and the power of intent. This in itself can open up doors for you to increase soulful ways of living.

Your life's purpose is not your career, though it may best be able to shine through it. Yet it is your job metaphorically, even your mission, should you choose to accept it, to know and revel in your life's purpose. It should fill you with joy and satisfaction, with a feeling of fitting you like a good pair of shoes. If your purpose seems like a job (paid or unpaid) you don't want, it probably isn't your life's purpose. Your life's purpose should be a like a job you love, given to you by your divinely inspired self.

Even if finding your individual purpose is tied to the Western mode of individualism, if you live in Western civilization, why not let yourself move in the morality of that culture? Western culture values individual expression, so why not take advantage of the collective archetypal power of shared thought and do your individual being? I used to feel that Eastern culture routinely had the better way of living and that I should be more Eastern in thought, always more communal and more Buddhist and unattached in my spiritual seeking. Now I feel that since I have lived in Western culture all my life, I might as well maximize those potentials and see them as no better or worse than any other way of being. All cultures have their shadows, and if I can be mindful (Eastern thought!) of the pitfalls, I may just be able to take the best and transmute (or accept) the worst.

Our true purpose vibrates with the essence of who we are, whether we have conscious thoughts about it or not. Perhaps only those who seek and those ready for some kind of change experience the difficult but rewarding task of finding their purpose. Having a sense of what purpose we are birthing can encourage us during hard times. This is the work of consciousness. Our true purpose then emerges as naturally and miraculously as when our bodies were formed in the womb. Our labor pains give birth to a conscious awareness of our part in the larger whole. We should treat our newfound awareness as tenderly as a mother moose treats her baby calf. If yours is a young vision, you should go easy on yourself. As it grows, you can put it to the task, supporting it with a knowing spirit. Everyone's true purpose is available and accessible. Is anything stopping you from finding, developing, or just enjoying yours?

I am once again tramping along old forest service bridges, this time deep in the accessible Bridger Mountains so near to my home in the Gallatin Valley. It is deep winter, and I am snowshoeing down a mild slope toward a winding stream. I do not expect to see moose; I only want to be in their environment. And there he is, to my left and ten yards away: a bull with paddles still intact, curled up in a huge ball, resting in an open patch right by the water. He has heard me coming; I am the only one raising my eyebrows in surprise. I've been enjoying my life purpose of loving and praising creation, and his lovely presence causes me to laugh out loud. He blinks. I don't. I gently back away, view him from a safer distance, and myself end up in a ball in the snow on a sunny winter morning, viewing him, the stream, and the cascading mountains surrounding us both. I love my job.

32

The Medicine of Conscious Prayer

Gone. Gone. Gone beyond. Gone beyond beyond. Hail the enlightened voyager!
—Sanskrit mantram

As a teenager, I used to walk into the formal Presbyterian church in the town where we lived with great curiosity. "Is God here?" I wanted to call out on Sunday mornings as the parishioners would take their seats and the minister would begin his serious, booming sermon. I would look around—up, mostly—sure that a lively God must dwell there if only I could open up to him or her. My dad seemed to like his religion, and I liked and admired my dad, so I figured that God must be there too. I liked our church and our minister; I just wasn't sure I wanted such a formal and quiet form of worship. Perhaps because I was a teenager, I needed a more dramatic experience, so I sought God in a noisier church, the Pentecostal. There I spoke in tongues, raised my hands, stomped my feet, prophesied, and found greed, adultery, and lecherous behavior right among my holy-rolling brethren. "Look to Jesus, not man," they would say. This I understood, but I still left that church, which seemed to have more men than God.

Later in life I found less religiously rigid paths. They helped me develop my own road of spirituality, one that also incorporated the sentience of nature. I began to realize that prayer was more like a state of consciousness than a series of requests naively offered up to a patriarchal god.

I discovered that many religions and spiritual paths contained similar methods of praying. One is the Medicine Wheel, a living, ancient ceremonial and divination tool used by indigenous peoples of many cultures. My particular introduction to one came as a result of my induction as an honorary member of the Wolf Clan of the Seneca Nation with Grandmother Twylah Nitsch as Elder. Although my time with the Senecas was brief, I later received extended teachings about the wheel from one of Grandmother Twylah's adopted children. While I recognize and respect the points of view of some tribal people who believe that these teachings are only for Native American people, I have been assured by the indigenous ones who taught me that their vision is more inclusive. They are completely convinced that the world's people need all the wisdom we can find, and the time is right for such sharing. I have accepted and learned from this philosophy.

The Medicine Wheel uses specifically chosen stones placed circularly in the seven major directions: East, South, West, North, the Within (center), the Above, and the Below. Incorporating certain ceremonial practices, a person using the wheel walks around it prayerfully to ascertain where the truth of his or her being resides. The truth varies in any given moment, depending on the teachings of the meanings surrounding each direction. For example, if I am just starting a new phase of my life, I may identify with and want to spend time in the East of the wheel (the place of new beginnings). If I am grieving and needing to let go, I will be drawn to stay in the West (the place of introspection and endings).

The psychological beauty I have discovered in the inherent power of the wheel is that it helps people know what they need: have they overstayed their welcome at a certain direction on the wheel, or are they rushing by it to avoid the fullness of the experience? The wheel is a self-regulating healing tool.

All forms of seeking a higher power that motivate us toward healed and full living can invite encouragement and enlightenment. As we remember to respect other beliefs, we paradoxically remember that we are all parts of the One. As we learn how to be spiritual beings having a human experience, we become, as my teacher Jacquelyn Small proclaimed, "practical mystics," able to take action in the world with inspiration.

In my own spiritual journey, I have found that theosophy alone couldn't heal the split in my heart. Nature, on the other hand, offered an impartial strength with no guilt. I never felt wrong sitting by a stream or under the arms of a fir tree. Even lightning doled out its hot hand near me without malice. However, as I moved through the process of learning to trust and then love nature, I began to believe that GOD-NATURE-SPIRIT was good and that we humans were bad. Years later, when I began to do my own healing, I realized how the shaming I'd received in my early life had taught me to believe that. At that point I instinctively knew that I would only fully heal by walking deeper into my own humanity-shadow, judgments and all. Luckily, I found the courage to do so from the love and acceptance of other wise human souls who did not coddle but who held me accountable to do my best while modeling that same integrity in their own lives.

I identify prayer as asking God for something and conscious prayer as the awareness of God in the moment with intent for everyone's highest good. What is the connection, then, between healing your innermost self and conscious prayer? As you heal, you free yourself of judgments that cloud your ability to pray consciously. Conscious prayer is less concerned with asking for things than with paying attention. It looks around with the eyes and senses of the physical body and says, "I will do what is needed this moment," and "I will bless the world."

Some years ago a local minister skeptical of my rather global spirituality narrowed his eyes and demanded to know how often I prayed. I laughed and said, "All the time! If God created everything, isn't everything prayer?" Every time I grieve someone's hurt, misfortune, or death, I am in conscious prayer. When I read the news and see another form of violence, I connect with my own darkness to remove judgment and then pray for a better way. Nature always helps us connect to our spiritual selves. When we interact with wild creatures and their habitats, we begin to understand our place in the universe a bit more. It is then that we are praying. Every moment we are aware of God and our heart listens, we are in a state of conscious prayer. When I am remembering who I really am, a child of God, and I see a hawk or make my grocery list or step into my car, I am in prayer. Any time we see, or hear, or smell, or taste, or feel anything that reminds us of God, we are in that same type of prayer, because we are in loving contact with the heart and mind of creation. Could we conceive of a life lived in such balance that conscious prayer becomes aware of praying to itself? Perhaps then the circle will be finally unbroken, and as Chief Joseph said, we "will fight no more forever." That the circle be unbroken is something to pray about, to visualize, and to realize that we can be in constant conscious prayer. It is up to us.

A moose wanders by the road I have been aimlessly strolling along today. She crosses only a few feet in front of me, glancing over casually, and then slides down the slope into the waiting meadow. I move into immediate conscious prayer with her, linking my soul to hers, and feel the heartbeat of Creation in us both. I pray and settle into the heart of God.

33

The Grandmothers and Grandfathers

I can see them, not with the eyes of my body, but with the eyes of my spirit.
—Anonymous

I am not sure when I was first truly aware of a group of benevolent unseen beings hovering in a circle above me; maybe it was a decade ago in Tucson, during my initial visit there, when I began to discover ancient places which had stories to tell. I'm also not sure how long the "unseen ones" had been with me before I really knew them, but now I know and appreciate them quite well.

But I get ahead of myself.

She was sixty-five, securely ensconced in her California home, and dying, her left side paralyzed and muscles in atrophy. Her mouth sagged on the left side, though her mind was as sharp as ever. An inoperable brain tumor, we were told. Nothing to do but wait. So we waited, my dad, my sister, and I. I sang to my mother in those last days, rubbed her feet with oil pressed from my garden flowers, and prayed, supplicating for a good passageway as she met the other side. Also inoperable was the minimal relationship I'd had with her. As I had grown into my own adulthood, I had claimed space apart from the sting of her words and the memory of her physical and emotional abuse. Now I was coming back for the last time to soften my own words and say goodbye. On her behalf, I fervently wished the indigenous concept of a good death, an easy journey. No one, no matter what has been done or left undone, deserves to suffer. It was easier to forgive when I saw her helpless state; my complete lack of judging her was the closest form of Christ-consciousness I had ever known. In my last visit with her, even though she was the one dying, I somehow understood in my own body Jesus' suffering, his cry to God, and his death.

Even with my dad's ineffable care of her, she was impatiently waiting to be able to slip into unconsciousness. During our last few days, in halting phrases she asked for the first time about my spirituality and did not discount it. I shared what I knew and had experienced. She listened intently, wide-eyed and wondering. I tried to help prepare her to "go to the light" and to release herself to the Great All, in whom she had never believed. I stayed with her for a week. As Dad wheeled her out of the family room and we had our last look at each other, she broke into pitiful crying. I felt numb. How do you say good-bye when you know it's the last time?

I traveled back home to Montana. Three nights later my dad called to inform me that she lay dying. That evening I hiked to an open spot on the east edge of town in the aptly named Story Mountains, which overlook my little town of Bozeman. After pouring out her story and mine to them, I began praying and singing for her. I supplicated to whoever in the spirit world would listen, whoever would be there to receive my prayers and receive her as well. It was that evening, as the sun was setting in the gentle Story Mountains, that I first looked up into the darkening sky and simply said "Oh." I saw in my mind's eye a group of eleven or twelve ancient beings that looked like seasoned Native American human spirits who had some mission to accomplish. I began singing in a foreign language unfamiliar to me—"tongues," as Pentecostal Christians would say—a gift I retained even beyond my Christian allegiances. But these tongues seemed to turn into a contemporary language of sorts and felt Native. Focusing now on the elders above me, I kept singing the same song over and over again, in a language I'd never heard before. As the sun dipped below the Tobacco Root Mountains, I fell silent. I could "see" these beings then, whisking away faster than the eye could follow, over to the west and down south, just where I imagined geography would place my parents' home many states away. I again "saw" the bright beings hovering over the roof right above her darkened bedroom, and there they stayed. Several minutes later, I felt released and relieved. Their image faded. I stood up to go, walking pensively back to my car and driving slowly back to my own home with soft porch lights waiting. My part, whatever it had been, was done. I later found out that my mother had slipped into unconsciousness that night and passed the next morning.

The following week, I was visiting with a Crow Indian friend and asked her if I could sing snatches of the song I'd been calling out on my mother's behalf the night she began to pass over. We settled onto a bench and I sang it to her. She looked at me with a hard blink. "Robyn," she said, "that is our Crow song of endings. We always sing it when somebody dies." I sighed and she took my hand. We sat that way together a long time.

I don't remember that song anymore, but it doesn't matter. It happened. I still often see what a Native friend said should rightly be called "the Grandmothers and Grandfathers." In fact, I remember how surprised I was when I first saw them again. I was in Tucson for the second time, back to the sensual desert so full of deep, pungent smells. It was early evening, a warm winter night, and I was in a state of meditation at a waterfall behind the lovely Ventana Canyon Resort. Suddenly they were there—some laughing, others nodding, and all with a great sense of humor and ceremony. "Whoa," I chortled in my thought-speech toward them. "I thought you were just for Mom." "No," I imagined they beamed back at me. "We're here for you. We belong to you, and you to us. We're here for your whole life. And we've all been together before, with you as part of us. We're here to encourage you in your life now, because we're not all together on the earth plane anymore."

I was in awe and listened. They told me many miraculous things that night, all of which I've forgotten, like I usually do in miraculous moments. But in the process they convinced me that they were for real and that they could be accessed whenever I thought of them. And so I do, and have, and continue to, whenever a moment of grace descends and I remember to turn my consciousness in their direction. I think they turn their consciousness toward me all the time. For that I am grateful and give thanks.

We all have these kinds of beings ready and waiting to encourage us through this impossible task of life. This type of gift is surely available to anyone who seeks and needs it. I could not conceive of the earth and heavens operating any other way. It is so natural, just the way moose meander in and out of a cool streambed on a late summer day. So if you are not too afraid, or are hesitant but willing to push through the fear, may you be open to sing your own songs. May you seek to know the invisible ones who love you just as much as or more than any human love you've ever known. Then try to remember what they tell you in the midst of your own amazement. Take this knowledge deep from the heart of your own instinctive nature and bring it back out to all your human relations, not by trying to be anything special, but simply by being who you really are. Then you will have and be able to share your own form of Moose Medicine.

May your own nature align with earth, the cosmos, and all the possibilities to come, and may you continue to proceed through the rest of your life and beyond with your own sure footsteps.

Epilogue

Now I see the secret of the making of the best persons. It is to grow in the open air, and to eat and sleep with the earth.
—Walt Whitman

Throughout this book, I've sought to chronicle the human passages of despair and joy while showing how nature has the ability to inspire as well as to heal what ails us. I have come to respect that nature does not have to match a human template in order for us to understand and benefit from its many offerings, from late red sunsets to moose woofing in the willows in the early morning.

All I ultimately know is that the thrill of being close to a live moose in the woods feeds my spirit and soul. It is a feast of the senses, a giving over of self to the Great All that enlivens and sustains. And my prayer for you is that you have found, or are finding, your own form of Moose Medicine to enrich your life.

My own life has come full circle, from an immature happiness to unexpected hardship to a maturing acceptance of all of life. I have learned to be content more often with reality as it is in the present moment. I am discovering how to be happy with what I have while still holding a place for yet unfulfilled dreams. I have also learned to allow grief its proper time and space without inviting it to overstay its welcome. Both moose and loving human teachers have shown me how to thrive. They have taught me how to increasingly live in the moment, to glory in the ineffable presence of nature even through suffering, and to love and approve of myself in all seasons.

Nature has many lessons to teach us, and it awaits our rapt attention. We need only show up and surrender to its benign essence. We are wise to heed its fierce teachings. Alone in nature, falling silent, leaving our familiar lives to meet our deeper familiars, we are reminded again of how to find the steady pulse of the spirits of trees and animals, plants, and sky. Becoming careful stewards and maintaining a deep relationship to all living entities remains our only salvation. We desperately need to remember this simple wisdom.

Once we understand the importance of wild ecosystems, we see the essential reasons to save, protect, and preserve natural places. In preservation, we are saving the "other," which is a telling reflection of ourselves. We nurture the deep heart of relationship within and without if we can save other creatures and landscapes unselfishly, protecting and cherishing the earth inhabitants who have always been our teachers. Moose have been my personal medicine, my reminders for living a life in sync with all that surrounds western Montana, the home that has supported my many natural and supernatural encounters.

The natural world revels both in and all around us. That which we learn from without becomes our teacher within. That which we learn within affects that without. Animals, plants, and stones offer themselves for our deepened understanding. As we renew in nature for any healing we need, we are able to more clearly see and know our own humanity. As we befriend our human darkness, our light enlarges to hold and transform it. We authentically live in truth, passing through each stage of life with increasingly authentic grace.

My fervent hope and prayer is that we will each do our part to assist a planetary shift into this transformation, our wisest calling.

When I begin to lose heart about the world and think that true human progress is only a wishful dream, I remember the works of famous ancient as well as contemporary mystics, quantum physicists, and ordinary people who have inspired me with their extraordinary wisdom. I take realistic comfort that even a small, sentient population may be enough to steer us toward higher realization.

A contemporary singer, Kenny Loggins, in the midst of his own awakening, wrote a song I have played for soulful seekers at the close of several workshops I've offered. It reminds me that we keep learning from a power greater than any of us alone, and yet it lives in each of us fully. He tells us that "we can all know everything without ever knowing why," reminding my own questioning mind that when it reaches the edge, it can indeed rest in the Great Mystery.

It's in every one of us to be wise
Find your heart
Open up both your eyes
We can all know everything
Without ever knowing why
It's in every one of us
By and by …

With consciousness, we have all we need to survive.
Nature provides the respite for us to thrive.
Blessings, and I'll be seeing you deep in the heart of your own natural being.

Acknowledgments

Many people have supported the creation of this book. To each and every one, I extend my thanks, even to those whose names do not appear here.

Gratitude to my long-time friend Eileen Wallin, who has always reminded me of who I really am, who listens with incredible depth, and always offers timely wisdom. Thanks to Deb McGill, the Bitterroot Mountains property manager who became a dear friend through providing months of cabin lodging. She shared her own deep connection to the moose I grew to love, as well as faithfully reading my manuscripts. I thank her grown children Kasey and Carrie for intuiting what became our magical "Moose Clan" gatherings. To my superb writing group members Ginny Watts-Chase (author, psychotherapist, and World Dance artist) and Barbara McGowan (artist and author of *A Brush With Nature*), I offer my deep appreciation for their dedicated attention to my work and their intelligent suggestions.

In memoriam, I send loving-kindness to my now-passed-over father for his unwavering belief in me and for introducing me to the beauty of nature through our quiet early morning summer walks at Lake Tahoe throughout my childhood.

Gratitude to the many readers who perused this manuscript over the years it was coming into form and being revised: Dr. Holcomb Johnston, Pam Pride, Debra Ramsdell, Margie Chase, Jill Davis, Meg Cook, Tracy Antonelli and her former husband Larry Bailey, who honored me as their psychological consultant of their brilliant equine program, Kristy

McFetridge, Pat Craig, Valerie Harms, my sister Karin Anderson (who recently lost her brave battle with cancer), and her intrepid daughter Kristina, who enthusiastically read my work. Last but not least, I am indebted to my private practice clients, whose inspired responses encouraged the completion of this book.

For excellent manuscript evaluations and writing coaching, I thank Molly May of Bozeman, Montana. Her thorough and crisp attention to the heart and soul of this work shaped the final stages. Any literary shortcomings found here are solely my own. To the project managers, editors, design team, and publishers of Balboa Press I extend my appreciation for doing their jobs so well.

For psychological and spiritual teachings, I extend my gratefulness to the many authors, teachers, and healers who have graced my life with goodness. Gratitude to David Whyte, John O'Donahue, Linda Star Wolf, Maori teacher Arapata, Sue Jane White, Jacquelyn Small, Thomas Moore, Bill Plotkin, Marion Woodman, Jean Houston, Jean Shinoda-Bolen, Grandmother Twylah, Carolyn Myss, Sam Keen, Angeles Arrien, the teaching staff at JFK University Transpersonal Psychology Department, Energy Management Coach Victoria Post, Sandra Ingerman, David Abrams, Vickie Molinar-Sanz, and the ageless wisdom of writers and poets Rumi, Rilke, Pablo Naruda, John Muir, and Walt Whitman, who have left an enduring legacy.

My deepest gratitude extends to the Spirit that unites us all, with whom we surely crafted this lovely earth, and to the moose who so generously moved into my life with the exact teachings I needed to live a soulful life. I am eternally yours.

About the Author

Robyn Bridges has been traversing the field of health and wholeness for over twenty years. A transpersonal teacher, mentor, speaker, and soul-based psychotherapist, she invites those seeking greater inner wisdom to find their own true north. She offers experience in Breathwork, Voice Dialogue, personal retreats, and body-mind-spirit counseling in person or by phone. Also providing outdoor meditation retreats, including ceremony in nature, Robyn assists seekers to honor the landscapes of their own life stories and how they fit into the collective progression. Through her business, Regenesis: Cultivating the Inner Landscape, she also provides a forty-unit, state approved program of Self-Directed Study in Psychology and Spirituality.

In addition to her Master's Degree in Counseling, Robyn holds certifications in Integrative and Shamanic Breathwork, EMDR, Advanced Hypnotherapy, Reiki Hands-On Healing, Wolf Clan Teachings, and the art of Feng Shui. She holds licenses as a Transpersonal Teacher and Spiritual Counselor through the Association for the Integration of the Whole Person (AIWP) and as a Professional Clinical Counselor in Montana (LCPC). Robyn has been given the name "She Who Knows the Way" through honorary membership in the Wolf Clan of the Seneca Nation.

Robyn has been a guest speaker for women's business groups, community functions, retreat weekends, and wellness-oriented radio shows. She has facilitated workshops in her home state of Montana, nationwide, and in Western Europe. During each, she reminds seekers that "the way out is through" and that nature is replete with personal messages of regeneration, renewal, and sustenance.

She also teaches local and long-distance classes based on *Moose Medicine* and her CD workshop *The Return of the Sacred Feminine,* as well as upcoming books *Two-Legged Medicine, Turtle Medicine,* and *This Way to the Kiva.* She lives in Bozeman, Montana, in the beautiful Valley of Flowers. Her books and CDs can be ordered through www.amazon.com. Robyn can be reached for speaking engagements or consulting at (406) 595-2410.

Terms of Transpersonal Living

All definitions are the author's compilation of developments in the Transpersonal Field of Psychology. Note that authors listed can be found in the Sources section.

Deep Ecology

Deep Ecology is the ethical and philosophical framework for a personal, communal, and collective way of life based on the importance and equality of all life forms. A term coined by Arne Ness in the seventies, it has since enjoyed increasing international scientific, social, academic, naturalist, and economic study of how to live in harmony with all life.

Ego

Ego is the self-aware function in human thinking and discernment of differences between self and other. A vital component of the psyche, ego houses our self-esteem and ability to feel success in the world, in relationships, and in work. Though much denigrated in some New Age groups today, the ego is actually crucial to our well-being. Its healthy development is necessary in developing our sense of self as a distinct member of society, in making daily decisions, and in realizing ourselves as individuals responsible to the whole. An unhealthy ego has too much or too little sense of self and prohibits the person from self-actualizing. Though an ultimate spiritual goal may be to park our egos at the door in order to reach transcendent states, we cannot release what we haven't developed! Forming and then balancing a healthy ego with a greater infusion of spirit can help us function at a higher level. (Authors Abraham Maslow, Debbie Ford, Dawna Markova)

Healing

Healing psychology is the act of the understanding, compassion, and acceptance required to be comfortable, complete, and self-actualizing in mind, body, spirit, and soul. Regardless of the specific healing method or technology employed, love is the primary teacher. The healing of psyche, ego, and spirit allows a revisit of past wounds and decisions made in order to readdress them in a safe and compassionate environment and in a type of relearning of positive parenting. "To heal is to feel" and "The way out is through" are two principles that lead to effective healing and an authentic life. Along the way, a sense of spirit is encouraged to develop, which inspires and helps individuals to resource themselves to a higher power. (Authors and their respective teaching programs: Jacquelyn Small, Linda Star-Wolf, and Robyn Bridges)

Health, Disease, and Healing Mandates

One shadow use of New Age healing can imply that a person is supposed to heal by recognizing the error in his or her thinking or actions. The Eastern term *karma* (one's personal destiny as set in motion by one's choices) can be used as a cloak disguising projected and unhealed guilt. Has the person with a cancer diagnosis been told (directly or indirectly) that he or she is not spiritually or mentally enough (conscious enough, penitent enough, believing enough)? How does compassion live in such a guilt-ridden state? Certain New Age groups who began with this type of original New Age thinking have evolved to a more compassionate and less judgmental stance and now say, "Sometimes we heal, and sometimes we don't." We can do our best to attend to all aspects of ourselves as we attempt to heal, but sometimes the Great Mystery has the last say. Bad things happen to good people, and vice-versa. The term "Beyond New Age" refers to a higher form of love that releases expectations that are really based on guilt. It invokes compassion as the healing salve. This paradigm is increasingly referred to as the Consciousness Movement.

Meditative Centering

Meditative centering emphasizes the importance of clearing the mind, body, and emotions to become fully present, attentive, and open. The act of meditation naturally centers the person; outer thoughts, actions, and concerns eventually fall away, and the person becomes present to himself and, if in an intentional group, to those around him as well as to the natural environment. (Authors Jack Kornfeld, Songyal Rinpoche, the Dali Lama)

New Age

The recent New Age movement formed from growing awareness of the astrological and spiritual significance of humanity's movement from the Picean Age (of developed individualism) to the Aquarian Age (of harmony and sharing). New Age thinking incorporates all spiritual paths that emphasize Oneness, unity, and peace. The light, or conscious side, of the New Age movement sincerely reaches for ultimate spiritual truth, personal balance of male and female qualities, global care and understanding, and a deep care for and responsibility toward the earth and her resources. The dark, or unconscious, side encourages narcissism, repeats religious judgment and guilt, and can contain cult pressure to conform in the same manner as the movements from which it seeks freedom.

Psyche

Psyche is the soulful organizing principle of the self that helps us to function in our daily lives through experiencing order and meaning. A damaged psyche has been abused in some manner and is unable to cope or to make sense of the realities of the world. A well psyche is vibrant, creative, relaxed with self and others, houses an intact ego, and understands boundaries. The healthy psyche can develop to the point of being able to release the ego at will in order to merge with the spiritual

Oneness in all things. The psyche is a living and enduring archetype, and a human blueprint arranging our mental, emotional, spiritual, and physical interactions. (Authors Jacquelyn Small, Founder and Director of Eupsychia, Carl Jung, Marion Woodman)

Shamanic Healing

Shamanic healing embodies the ancient practice of becoming "other" in order to heal physical, spiritual, or emotional illness. In tribal societies, shamans are trained through a lineage. They are sometimes referred to as holy ones, whose living needs are taken care of by the tribe. In modern times, though shamans of lineage still exist and do their work, a broader use of shamanic skills is being developed by ordinary people who have experienced the energy of transformation into other human, animal, and elemental energies. Many contemporary healers and therapists utilize shamanic energy when helping clients to be free of entities; some use the energy to simply understand how the client feels in his or her own body, to increase awareness and compassion toward the client, and to provide a greater sense of accompaniment in the one receiving the healing work. This work can include Soul Retrieval, a calling back of lost parts of the person's inner psychic configuration that were lost in some kind of trauma. Use and maintenance of ethical boundaries in all aspects of shamanic healing are essential.

Soul

A person's soul is the invisible creative force emanating from spirit and expressed through the psyche, which carries a profound sense of desire and longing. As esoteric teachings remind us, the soul does not care if the person is happy or sad; it just wants to feel and to have both personal and relational experience. Soul is developed through a willingness to enter into both the bliss of joy that elevates and the fire of suffering that burns through us. The development of soulfulness tends to be seen in a person willing to live with, express, and embrace these opposites. (Authors Thomas Moore, James Hillman, Depak Chopra)

Spirit

Spirit is the life force all living things contain before birth, during life, and after death. Spirit infuses our human identity with a sense of a home beyond the confines of the earth, yet while we are embodied it seeks to intertwine with our psyche like a second strand of DNA, one not complete without the other. Spirit is the Creator, the Great Mystery, the All That Is, God/ Goddess-force that infuses our lives with meaning, inspiration, and a felt sense of the bigger picture. Spiritual wisdom is thought to come through the individual's Higher Self, which develops and refines through consciousness and experience. Though all spiritual paths contain human values, they tend to be less structured and less insistent on compliance than religious organizations, the latter of which require adherence to certain moral values and may or may not contain a sense of spirituality. (Authors Angeles Arrien, John O'Donahue, Matthew Fox)

Transpersonal Psychology

Transpersonal psychology is the study of our larger human potential and the belief that we are multifaceted human beings—more than just our human selves. It includes a respect for the earthly as well as spiritual experiences a person may have and has been the primary forerunner of the current, popular "body/mind/spirit" approach. The International Transpersonal Association (ITA) sponsors yearly conferences worldwide where people of many cultures connect. A few of the major original developers in the field with whom I have studied or know their works are Thomas Moore, Angeles Arrien, Marion Woodman, David Whyte, Depak Chopra, Stan and Christina Grof, Jacquelyn Small, Ken Wilbur, Sam Keen, Clarissa Pinkola Estes, Carol Pearson, Debbie Ford, Jean Shinoda Bolen, Matthew Fox, Brian Swimme, Fritzjof Capra, and Rupert Sheldrake.

Recommended Readings

Abram, David. *The Spell of the Sensuous.* New York: Random House, 1997. ISBN 0-67977639-7. A fascinating look at nature and our sensory capabilities, creating a language of exploration of environmental activists, scientists, and scholars to enliven a felt sense of intertwining the sensate with all other life forms, including the earth itself. *Becoming Animal.* New York: First Vintage Books, Random House, 2011. ISBN 978-0- 375-71369-9. Challenges the technical unconsciousness of our times and exhorts the return to our original instinctive kinship with our bodies and the earth.

Abrams, Jeremiah. *The Shadow in America.* Novato, Calif.: Nataraj Publishing, 1994. ISBN 1-882591-17-8. A revealing look at the underbelly of American politics. Abrams is founder/director of Mount Vision Institute, Fairfax, California. Offers other books, workshops, international thematic travel.

Barbato, Joseph, and Lisa Weinerman, editors. *Heart of the Land: Essays on Last Great Places.* New York: Pantheon Books and The Nature Conservancy, 1994. ISBN 0-679-43508-5. A fine collection of essays about a variety of wild places.

Bolen, Jean Shinoda, M.D. *Goddesses in Older Women.* Quill, an imprint of Harper Collins Publishers, 2002. ISBN 0-06-019152X.

Bolen is the author of several books detailing archetypes in men, women, and the collective unconscious.

Capra, Fritjof. *The Turning Point: Science, Society, and Rising Culture*. New York: Bantam Books, 1983. ISBN 0-553-01480-3. Though published twenty years ago, this book is a basic primer on quantum physics and the miraculous connections between science and spirit.

Devall, Bill, and George Sessions. *Deep Ecology: Living as if Nature Mattered*. Salt Lake City: Gibbs Smith/Peregrine Smith Books, 1985. ISBN 0-87905-247-3. A landmark piece defining the depths of what deep ecology means.

Doyle, Brian. *Mink River*. Corvallis, OR: Oregon State University Press. 2011. ISBN 978-0-87071-585-3. A superbly engaging style of writing that incorporates all our human and divine sensing about the inner and outer nature of a small Oregon town through Native American and Irish eyes.

Duerk, Judith. *Circle of Stones: A Woman's Journey to Herself*. San Diego, CA: Lura Media, 1989. ISBN 0-931055-66-0. A much-needed book even today to help us understand how the feminine thrives both in solitude and in community.

Emoto, Dr. Masaru. *Messages from Water*. Tokyo: HADO Publishing, 1999. ISBN 908074213- 9. Photos and text showing water's response to human and environmental influences. As shown in the movie "What the Bleep Do We Know?"

Ford, Debbie. *The Dark Side of the Light Chasers*. New York: Riverhead Books, 1998. ISBN 1-57322-096-5. A revealing and effective book on how to deal with the human shadow.

Forward, Susan. *Emotional Blackmail.* New York: Harper Collins, 1997. ISBN 0-06-0187573. Provides insight about intentional use of emotions and how to break free of dysfunctional patterns.

Keen, Sam. *Faces of the Enemy: Reflections of the Hostile Imagination.* New York: Harper and Row, 1988. ISBN 0-06-250467-3. A valuable account of how we create a national "shadow" to keep the enemy "out there" rather than see the "enemy within." A good companion to Dawna Markova's *No Enemies Within.*

Louv, Richard. *The Nature Principle: Human Restoration and the End of Nature-Deficit Disorder.* Chapel Hill, NC: Algonquin Books of Chapel Hill, 2011. The first to identify our technological and societal ills as originating from "Nature Deficit Disorder," this compelling report combines research and personal stories elucidating this real problem and its necessary solution.

Markova, Dawna. *No Enemies Within.* Berkeley: Conari Press, 1994. ISBN 0-943233-64-X. An excellent book to help with numerous exercises to develop self-esteem and personal comfort with "shadow" issues.

McLuhan, T.C. *The Way of the Earth: Encounters with Nature in Ancient and Contemporary Thought.* New York: Simon & Schuster, 1994. ISBN 0-671-75939-6. A collection of nature essays from a wide variety of scholarly and interactive experience.

Metzner, Ralph. *Green Psychology: Transforming Our Relationship to the Earth.* Rochester, VT: Park Street Press, 1999. ISBN 0-89281-798-4. A groundbreaking book exploring global pathology and the path of restoration of our relationship with nature.

O'Donahue, John. *Anam Cara: A Book of Celtic Wisdom.* New York: Cliff Street Books/Harper Collins, 1997. ISBN: 0-06-018279-2. A beautiful, poetic, lyrical read by an intelligent and heart-felt Irish former priest who offered Irish travel adventures, sometimes along with poet David Whyte. O'Donahue passed away suddenly in January of 2007; his loss has been mourned worldwide.

Oliver, Mary. *Dream Work*. New York: Atlantic Monthly Press, 1986. ISBN 0-87113-071-8. Award-winning poems relating humans to the natural world.

Plotkin, Bill. *Soulcraft: Nature and the Sacred: Crossing into the Mysteries of Nature and Psyche*. Novato, CA: New World Library, 2003. ISBN 1-57731-422-0. An invigorating experience of the journey of the human soul and the passages necessary to help us along the way that the heart of nature provides. *Nature and the Human Soul: Cultivating Wholeness and Community in a Fragmented World*. Novato, CA: New World Library, 2008. Defines and describes the archetypes of eight stages of human life, moving us from the ego-centric to soul-centric awareness. A manifesto for growth and mature change.

Rilke, Rainer Maria. *Selected Poems of Rainer Maria Rilke*. Translated by Robert Bly. New York: Perennial Library/Harper and Row, 1981. ISBN 0-06-090727-4. A lovely translation of some of Rilke's most popular poems.

Romanyshyn, Robert. *The Soul in Grief: Love, Death, and Transformation*. Berkeley: Frog Ltd., 1999. ISBN 1-55643-315-8. A powerful, frank account of one man's long journey back from the brink of despair after the passing of his wife.

Ryrie, Charlie. *The Healing Energies of Water*. Boston, MA: Journey Editions, 1999. ISBN 1-885203-72-1. A culturally and textually supportive look, with photos, at water's many conscious and magnificent healing properties. Inspiring and informative.

Rumi, Jalaluddin. *We Are Three*. Translated by Coleman Barks. Athens, Georgia: Maypop Books, 1987. ISBN 0-9618916-0-2. A collection of several of Rumi's best poems.

Sams, Jamie, and David Carson. *Medicine Cards* (packet and book). Santa Fe, New Mexico: Bear and Co, 1988. ISBN 0-939680-53-X. Realistic, positive readings for personal insight. Also author of *Sacred Path Cards*. Jamie also is a Wolf Clan member of the Seneca Nation..

Schneider, Michael. *The Beginner's Guide to Constructing the Universe: Mathematical Archetypes of Nature, Art and Science*. New York: Harper Perennial, 1995. ISBN 0-06-092671-6. A fascinating exploration of the spiritual and synchronistic relationships within and between numbers and their evidence in nature.

Sheldrake, Rupert. *The Rebirth of Nature: The Greening of Science and God*. Rochester, Vermont: Park Street Press, 1994. ISBN 0-89281-510-8. A ground-breaking look at how science and spirituality are interconnected.

Small, Jacquelyn. *Psyche's Seeds: The Twelve Sacred Principles of Soul-Based Psychology*. New York: Jeremy Tarcher/Putnam, 2001. ISBN 1-58542-096-4. *Awakening in Time*. Austin, TX: Eupsychian Press, 1991. ISBN 0-939344-18-1. Author of several esoteric and cutting-edge books on human transformation.

Somé, Malidoma Patrice. *Ritual: Power, Healing, and Community*. Portland, Ore.: Swan/Raven and Co., 1993. ISBN 0-9632310-2-2. African speaker at many conferences worldwide, with degrees from the Sorbonne and Brandeis University.

Sounds True. *Learning Tapes for the Inner Life*. One of the most established tape/CD/interview articles of current work offered in catalog. 1-800-333-9185. www.soundstrue.com.

Storr, Anthony. *Solitude: A Return to the Self.* New York: Free Press/ Macmillan, 1988. BF637.S64S65. Extols the power of solitude to enhance creativity and relieve depression.

Swan, James, editor. *The Power of Place: Sacred Ground in Natural and Human Environments.* Wheaton, Ill.: Quest Books, 1991. ISBN 0-8356-0670-8. A global look at the magic that special places hold for people and cultures.

Teale, Edwin Way, editor. *The Wilderness World of John Muir.* Mariner Book, Houghton Mifflin, New York, 2001. ISBN 0-618-12751-8. An engaging read of some of Muir's most exciting adventures and his deep connection with nature.

Walsh, Roger, and Frances Vaughan. *Beyond Ego.* Los Angeles: Jeremy Tarcher, 1980. ISBN 0-87477-175-7. Provides an excellent background in transpersonal psychology and the nature of consciousness.

Whyte, David. *The House of Belonging.* Langley, WA: Many Rivers Press, 1997. ISBN: 0-9621524-3-9. A moving collection of poems about the many ways we discover we belong. *What To Remember When Waking.* CD collection: Boulder, CO: Sounds True, 2010. 800-333-9185.

CPSIA information can be obtained at www.ICGtesting.com
Printed in the USA
LVOW12s0353190814

399747LV00004B/238/P